Food Retail Management Strategic Cases

Dr. Russell J. Zwanka

Author of

A Marketing Manual for the Millennium

Customer Connectivity in Global Brands and Retailers

Requisite Reading for the Renaissance Retailer

Operating in the New Cuba

Would You Shop Here if You Didn't Work Here?

Customers First. Profits Second.

ISBN-13: 978-1523255009

ISBN-10: 1523255005

About the Author

Dr. Russell J. Zwanka is a Marketing Professor at the State University of New York at New Paltz, and is also CEO of Triple Eight Marketing, a retail consultancy- helping food organizations re-align around customer lifestyle and orientation. Dr. Z has led the merchandising, marketing, advertising, procurement, and all customer engagement areas for multiple food retail companies domestically and internationally.

Dr. Z holds a Doctorate in International Business from ISM in Paris, France. He also holds a Masters of Science in Management from Southern Wesleyan University, and a Bachelors of Science in Psychology from the University of South Carolina. Russell has spoken at various events, including the Carnegie Mellon Social Media Conference, the University of Manitoba Marketing Conference, the Argyle Executive Forum in New York City, and the New Paltz Chamber Buy Local Event.

Additionally, he has served on the IGA Retailer Advisory Board, the Consumer Goods Forum Marketing Committee, the Topco Operations Board, the Hudson Valley Community College School of Marketing Advisory Board, the Hudson Valley Economic Development Corporation Food and Beverage Alliance, the National Grocers Association University Coalition, and the Nielsen Retailer Advisory Committee. Russell can be followed at "Dr.Z@TEM888" and www.tripleeightmarketing.com.

Foreword

The art of food retail management in a company's home market is one of strategy, tactics, environmental awareness, intense competition and elicits the need to be quick to respond to external and internal variables. Once a company decides to move outside of its home market, an entirely new set of variables presents itself. Not only does the company need to perform the everyday functions of buying and selling goods or services; but it now must deal with being further from the home office, trying to attract a local consumer that may not inherently trust a company from the outside, and it must also understand the local employment situation and unique nuances of the local workforce.

Quite simply, everything matters. In this book, we will cull the best practices from some of the most successful consumer goods companies and food retailers in the world and put it all together into a "blueprint for success"- an operating guideline encompassing the "best of the best".

Table of Contents

Brand Connections

Every food retail company in the world connects in the same way- with their brand. How they go to market, how they engage customers, how they price their products, even how their company can connect on a "higher purpose"- all strategies, tactics, communications, and actions should be centered upon the brand message. Know your brand and you are heading in the right direction. Forget your brand and risk being over-taken by your competition. The world of food retail is tight on margins and heavy on traffic. If you are going to compete, you need an identity.

World marketing guru Kevin Lane Keller describes brands in the following manner:

"Brands....are a shorthand way for consumers to reduce risk. As life gets more complicated and consumers have less time, the ability of a brand to be a predictable experience is important, in that consumers will automatically return to the same brand."[1]

The total number of new global consumer goods products exceeds two hundred thousand per year. This means over five hundred forty products are released per day.[2] Why do brands and retailers need to connect with customers? Is it not enough to simply satisfy a basic need? In figure 2.1, Maslow's Hierarchy of Needs points to satisfying food and shelter as basic to human existence.

Branding, whether attached to a consumer goods product or to a retailer that sells the product, lifts the consumer up from the figure 2.1 "physiological" needs centered upon survival into the "esteem" and "self-actualization" levels of achievement, confidence, spontaneity, and respect by others. A brand, when positioned well, fulfills more than its base requirement for the consumer. The global population is increasingly becoming connected with each other through the internet. Even in remote Africa, the population is able to see how the rest of the world lives and aspire towards that type of status or living situation.[3]

Figure 2.1 Maslow's Hierarchy of Needs

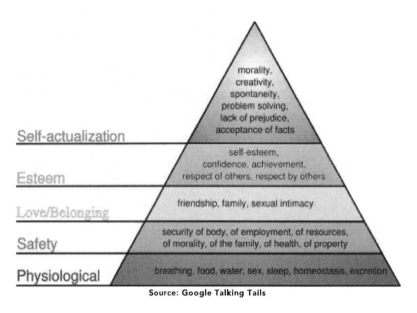

Source: Google Talking Tails

Hans G. Gueldenberg, Chief Executive Officer of Nestle Deutschland AG described branding as: "Brands are road signs that help people find orientation in the jungle of supply." Brands were further described as "personalities" and a "source of reputation that customers can trust."[4] With this level of impact, it would seem that there would be one straight-forward method of branding in the global marketplace. As we will see, the strategies and tactics differ by brand, by retailer, and by country.

Previously it was acceptable to solely provide superior products and distinctive functional benefits. But today's brands must also address process benefits (making transactions between buyers and sellers easier, quicker, and cheaper) as well as relationship benefits (rewarding the willingness of consumers to identify themselves and to reveal their purchasing behavior).[5]

Brand Touch points

All brands have multiple customer touch points. Touch points describe the various interaction points between the brand and the eventual consumer. Defined, a brand touch point is "all of the different ways that your brand interacts with, and makes an impression on, customers, employees, and other stakeholders. Every action, tactic and strategy you undertake to reach customers and stakeholders, whether it is through advertising, through your front-end cashiers, a customer service call, or a referral, represents a touch point."[6] These touch points can be in-person (holding the product in a store) or mentally (watching an ad on the television). The keen global brand marketers are aware of their brand touch points, and strategically address each touch point within the operating countries.

Traditional brand touch points to be measured and strategized:

1. **Brand awareness and brand recognition**- Provides direction as to whether the entire marketing mix is effectively getting your brand out to its target audience.
2. **Brand understanding**- Determines whether potential customers have knowledge about what your brand stands for, the value it provides, and the benefits that can accrue from experiences with your brand.
3. **Brand uniqueness**- Measures the degree of uniqueness that current and potential customers ascribe to your brand, especially as it relates to your adopted point of difference from other brands.
4. **Brand relevance**- Looks at how meaningful and relevant the value of your brand is to the various stakeholders it serves, based upon the marketplace needs, wants, and un-met desires.
5. **Brand credibility**- Measures whether current and/ or prospective customers find your brand's promise to be accurate and believable.
6. **Brand preference**- Measures to what extent customers prefer your brand to others within their potential consideration set and category.
7. **Brand consideration**- Helps make the link between brand preference and the degree to which customers are putting your brand into their final consideration set.
8. **Brand purchase conversion**- Measures the degree to which your brand is put into a final purchase consideration set and your ability to convert that consideration into a sale.
9. **Brand delivery**- Measures whether current and potential customers believe you are delivering upon and fulfilling your brand promise.
10. **Brand satisfaction**- Determines whether the brand lived up to expectations.
11. **Brand advocacy**- Measures and assesses those customers who are considered loyal to your brand and their willingness to put their reputation on the line by recommending your brand.[7]

Six more touch point metrics to consider are:

1. **Brand stretch-** Gets customers and other stakeholders to articulate where they believe the brand can or cannot stretch relative to new categories, opportunities, and geographies.
2. **Brand-driven customer acquisitions-** Depicts actual new customers you are attracting or acquiring as a result of your brand asset management efforts.
3. **Brand-driven customer retention-** Measures the number of customers you would have lost had you not activated a sound brand asset management strategy, providing understanding of the degree of loyalty that customers have to your brand.
4. **Brand share of wallet-** Measures the number of existing customers who are buying more products or services from you as a result of your brand building efforts.
5. **Brand price premium-** Determines the premium your brand is able to command over other competing brands within your category.
6. **Brand loyalty-** Measures if customers are coming back to your brand time and time again.[8]

In one McKinsey study, the connection between brand and customer was seen on three links: emotional relationship, purchase process, and product attributes. The study describes consumers as being influenced by emotional connections they form with products. Stated in the study, "Making the most of all touch points can reinforce an already powerful brand, help build an obscure or struggling brand, and limit the harm from a damaged one."[9]

Ultimately, what a retailer or consumer goods company brings to the global marketplace is their brand. As defined by Rowley, the brand is "a name, term, sign, symbol, design, or combination of these which is used to identify the goods or services of one seller or group of sellers and to differentiate them from these competitors."[10] The successful global brand emphasizes four aspects:

1. A brand is dependent upon customer perception.
2. Perception is influenced by the added-value characteristics of the product.
3. The added-value characteristics need to be sustainable.
4. Branding may be worldwide, but preferences are local.[11]

Brands have come a long way since being described as "a physical impression of ownership on livestock by way of hot-iron branding."[12] Brands are now reflected in how they connect with the end-user, or customer.

A modern definition of a brand is as follows: "Trade name: a name given to a product or service or a customer experience represented by a collection of images and ideas; often, it refers to a symbol such as a name, logo, slogan, and design scheme."[13] A familiar brand gives the sense that it is a proven entity. The customers know that the efficacy of the item(s), and the quality have already been proven and established. These facts, coupled with the speed of information, allow a clear opportunity to sink or swim as a brand very quickly. Lose the focus on quality and consistency or disappoint one loyal user, and the speed of the internet will pass the word on to thousands of customers within minutes. Reciprocally, live up to your promises, over-deliver on quality and effectiveness, and the speed of the internet becomes your friend.

It is clear that certain categories or commodities have brands that influence behavior more than others. Relevant to social media and its effect on brand influence, "technology and retail ranked highest, while insurance, utilities, and healthcare ranked lowest."[14] "Brands in the most-loved list tend to be aspirational, whereas those in the most-hated list tend to be functional or niche.", states Malcolm Wilkinson, partner at management consultancy Deloitte.[15] The brands that resonate with customers "excel at targeting and forging a strong connection with their market."[16]

Key Findings:

> Brands are a shorthand way for customers to reduce risk.
> A brand's touch points include every interaction the brand has with the consumers.
> A brand is defined by the *consumer's* interpretation, not necessarily the intended interpretation from the company.
> A consumer goods company or retailer must first establish its own identity before presenting to the public.
> The company's associates must be the "brand believers" who take the brand essence to the public.
> Possessing a clear identity is crucial before expanding into the global marketplace.

Discussion Questions

1. In Maslow's Hierarchy of Needs, how do brands relate to each level, and how can you apply that information to the food industry?
2. Is it better to have brand followers or brand advocates? Explain.
3. In a scenario where you are entering a new town with your store, describe the various brand touchpoints you would seek to address with your potential customers.
4. Where does the brand's real meaning lie, with the company or the customer? Explain.
5. Discuss the brand connection of Aldi versus the brand connection of Whole Foods.
6. What would you suggest to a retailer whose brand is centered upon fresh foods and foodservice and the local economy has just hit 12% unemployment?
7. What type of food retail outlet would you suggest to open in inner-city Detroit? Beverly Hills? Indianapolis?
8. Why is a trusted brand comforting to a customer?

Global Retailers

Consumers are said to want "the same, but different". They want the familiarity of the McDonald's golden arches, but they want to know they are in Canada or the United Kingdom or even Israel. A consistent brand can still be modified by market, in order to convey localization with its target customers. For example, the Spanish shoe company Camper changes its store décor by country. Sometimes the walls have writing from around the world, sometimes they have snapshots, and sometimes they are full of products. It does not matter the décor, the store's attitude and personality remain the same.[17]

It is important to understand the "place" of the retail establishment in each of the operating countries, as it will mean different things to different cultures. In Colombia, a gas station is the hub of the community; whereas in Japan, it solely serves as a place to functionally fill the vehicle with gas.[18] In Tel Aviv, Israel, the McDonald's golden arches have been replaced with a blue and white adaptation and an addition of the word "kosher" in Hebrew.[19]

As one study stated, "Retailers may have to define themselves not once but many times over. Retailers that rely on a single brand formula can find themselves forced out of some markets."[20]

As an additional example of the changing variables by locale, one McKinsey study on apparel shopping patterns in Brazil, China, and India involving dozens of focus groups, store visits, interviews, and shopping diaries; the following profound differences were found:

- ➤ Chinese have small budgets and small wardrobes.
- ➤ Indians show a strong preference for shopping with the family.
- ➤ Brazilian shoppers are fashion conscious and credit ready.[21]

Consider the issues of selling apparel in China versus selling it in India and Brazil. Rather than traditional methods of marketing products, studies suggest that retailers should utilize new approaches centered upon in-store merchandising and advertising. In addition, studies show a stark difference between the older demographic of shoppers and the young adults. China's apparel market (US$ 84 billion) is currently the world's third largest market, behind the United States at US$ 232 billion and Japan at US$ 100 billion. It is, however, by a large margin, the fastest growing apparel market in the world.[22]

In another example of global customer contrasts, China's consumers have small, undifferentiated wardrobes where 40 percent of respondents report wearing similar clothing at work, formal social occasions, and dates with friends and family. The number of 40 percent is compared to 8 percent in Brazil, 13 percent in India, and 11 percent in Russia.[23] Chinese apparel consumers do not place a premium on foreign brands, with only 25 percent responding that international brands offer better value than domestic brands. In India, the studies show that over 50 percent of consumers involved in studies say that international brands are superior in value or quality.

In India, the locals spend the same share of income on apparel as Brazilians and Chinese, but the shopping habits in India are drastically different. Nearly 40 percent of shoppers stated that shopping revolved around special occasions, weddings, and religious festivals. In India, shopping is a family activity, where nearly 70 percent of shoppers go to stores with family, and more than 74 percent (more than twice the average of Brazil, China, and Russia) see shopping as the best way to spend time with family.[24]

In Brazil, there are significant foreign retailer challenges, such as product demands that differ from those in the home market, a strong preference for local fashions, and the unique combination of widespread customer credit use and an un-developed credit market. Brazilians are extremely fond of shopping for apparel (almost 80 percent look forward to it). More than 60 percent of Brazilian shoppers think shopping for products on credit is fine. The fact that Brazilians are fine with debt has fueled incredible expansion of Brazil's credit industry in the last eight years. More than half of Brazilian shoppers say they use most of the clothing they buy for going out with friends and family, which is much higher than China, India, or Russia.[25] Clearly, any retailer operating in Brazil, Russia, India, and China must have varying merchandising and assortment by country and by demographic within each country.

In 2007, the combined sales of the top ten retailers grew by 7.2 percent, but their overall share of the top two-hundred fifty retailers shrunk slightly from 30.1 percent to 29.6 percent. Only two companies showed double-digit sales increases, as compared to six of the top ten in 2006.

The top ten retailers of 2007 were the following:

Top Ten Retailers 2007

Top 250 Rank	Company	Country of Origin	Sales (US$ mil)	Growth
1	Wal-Mart	U.S.	374,526	8.6%
2	Carrefour	France	112,604	5.5%
3	Tesco	UK	94,740	10.9%
4	Metro	Germany	87,586	7.2%
5	Home Depot	U.S.	77,349	-2.1%
6	Kroger	U.S.	70,235	6.2%
7	Schwarz	Germany	69,346	12.7%
8	Target	U.S.	63,367	6.5%
9	Costco	U.S.	63,088	7.0%
10	Aldi	Germany	58,487	5.7%

Source: Global Powers of Retailing 2009

On average, the top two-hundred fifty retailers operated in 6.7 countries, with an average of 21.3 percent of their total sales coming from outside their country of origin. Interestingly, retailers staying close to home grew at a rate of 2.0 percentage points higher than those that grew externally from their country of origin; but their composite net profit margin was 2.7 percent compared to 4.0 percent by those more globally-focused. These results are consistent year over year.[26]

Diversification across multiple countries and customer types consistently translates into the ability to augment slower sales or lower gross profit opportunities with higher growth rates and/ or profit opportunities. European and African/ Middle Eastern retailers tend to be more focused abroad than those from the United States or even Japan. Where European retailers had a presence in 11.1 countries, perhaps reflecting the relative homogeneity of Europe, Japanese retailers had a presence in just 2.8 countries. Germany reflected the highest external sales, with an average presence in 13.8 countries and 41.8 percent of their volume from foreign countries.[27]

Of the various commodities sold by the top two-hundred fifty global retailers, food makes up just over half of the total. Most of these food retailers are immense in volume (averaging US$ 19.1 billion in sales), and are present in an average of 4.9 countries and are realizing 23.4 percent of their sales from foreign sources.[28] When food companies decide to enter a market, they make their presence known, work to understand the local market, and quickly move to profitability when structured properly to reflect the local marketplace.

Not surprisingly, the emerging markets of Brazil, India, Russia, and China contributed tremendously to overall growth of the top retailers. In 2007, the fifty top growth retailers saw their sales grow at a composite rate of 28.7 percent, or 3.8 times faster than the rate for the entire group. The net gross profit margin was 4.5 percent versus 3.7 percent for the top two-hundred fifty. In the emerging markets, the majority of the companies are involved in food retailing. Many of the food retailers operated supermarkets, hypermarkets, and convenience stores.[29]

We will be analyzing the methods of international operating by Tesco, Carrefour, and Wal-Mart. These three retailers represent the top three retailers in the world, with a combined annual 2007 sales turnover of over US\$ 582 billion. These retailers were chosen for their success rates, international focus, and ability to adapt their operations to reflect the local marketplaces in which they operate; while also continuing their focus on aggregated buying power and international operating methods.

Also, not surprisingly, food expenditure per capita varies widely throughout the world. For example, the following are "one week" food expenditures throughout the world:

> Germany: \$500.07 USD per week or 375.39 Euros
> United States: \$341.98 USD per week
> Italy: \$260.11 USD per week or 214.36 Euros
> Mexico: \$189.09 USD per week 1862.78 Mexican pesos
> Poland: \$151.27 USD per week or 582.48 Zlotys
> Egypt: \$68.53 USD per week or 387.85 Egyptian Pounds
> Ecuador: \$31.55 USD per week
> Bhutan: \$5.03 USD per week or 224.93 nguitrum
> Chad: \$1.23 USD per week or 685 CFA francs[30]

The global retailers are primarily originating from North America and Western Europe. Wal-Mart is equal to the next four largest retailers combined, and has held the number one spot for more than ten years. Kroger is the largest traditional American grocer and the largest single-market grocery retailer in the world.[31]

The operations involved in bringing a retail format or company across national borders are intense, multi-variate, and complex. Not only does a company face stiff competition in its local market, but it enters each country eliciting the fiercest competitors in each market as well. The operating methods need to be honed considerably in the "home" or domestic market before venturing into the world to try selling merchandise against some of the best competition each country has to offer.

Key Findings:

> Customers want the brand consistency that comes from a well-established brand essence, plus they also want their local tastes and product needs to be reflected in the offering. This combination makes international retailing incredibly complex.

> In Colombia, a gas station is the hub of the community; whereas in Japan, it solely serves as a place to fill your vehicle with gas. This example shows the local knowledge needed in order to ensure that you understand your store's purpose and meaning in each marketplace.

> As another example, Indians spend the same share of income on apparel as Brazilians and Chinese, but their reasons for shopping are drastically different. Nearly 40 percent of Indians go apparel shopping for special occasions, weddings, and religious festivals, and nearly 70 percent of Indian shoppers go to the store with family members. These numbers are nearly double the rates in Brazil, China, and Russia.

> The top ten retailers in the world saw growth rates of around 7.2 percent in 2008. Wal-Mart, Carrefour, and Tesco make up US$ 582 billion in sales, and are the top three in the world. Wal-Mart annual revenue is as large as the next four retailers combined.

> Of the top two-hundred fifty retailers, over 50 percent of them are food retailers. Diversification allows the ability to grow in some markets while facing shrinking sales in other markets. This ability to spread sales volume over many different global markets is a key benefit to globalization.

> European and African/ Middle Eastern retailers tend to have a higher percent of their sales revenue coming from countries other than their home countries. German retailers realize 41.8 percent of their volume from foreign sources, and are present in an average of 13.8 countries. Japanese retailers are the lowest on these scales, with a presence in 2.8 countries.

- The net gross profit of global retailers averages 4.5 percent versus 3.7 percent in companies with primarily domestic businesses. This profit
- rate is another key benefit of global diversification. When approaching the BRIC (Brazil, Russia, India, and China) countries, a retailer stands to show tremendous sales gains, share gains, and profit gains.
- Food expenditure per capita ranges from US$ 500.07 per week in Germany to US$ 341.98 per week in the United States, and down to US$ 31.55 per week in Ecuador and US$ 1.23 per week in Chad.

Discussion Questions

1. Global retailers undertake a massive operation of principles, tastes, ethics, logistics, marketing, etc. Give one example of how you would structure your retail company to maximize its local opportunities for sales and profits.

2. Does bigger always mean better? Explain your answer with specifics.

3. Some retailers sell food, some sell apparel, some sell hardware. How do these commodity differences impact their operating procedures, and methods of going to market, by country?

4. Name a type of retailer you would want to set-up in Rio de Janiero, Moscow, Nigeria, and Mumbai. Explain two differences between each of theses retailers.

5. What are four strategies you would implement with a food retailer to help them compete in a differentiated way in the United States?

6. What are four strategies you would implement with a food retailer to help them compete in a differentiated way in Toronto?

7. From visiting a local food store, what are four suggestions you would make to increase sales?

8. From visiting a local food stores, what are four suggestions you would make to increase profits?

Global Retail Strategic Overview

Throughout the world, retailers are constantly developing and perfecting various methods to reach their customers, remain relevant, and stay ahead of the competition. In this segment, we will analyze a number of various global retail strategies, in order to discern those that work, and those strategies that need to be altered. This analysis should bring us towards an understanding of which methods are effective in ensuring that customers see these retailers as part of their community, and how that feeling offers a value to their shopping experience. In addition, ideas will be offered that can be replicated across geographies.

The economic malaise that hit the world's economy forced a shift in a number of strategies and tactics to make sure that customer needs are met while the economy stabilizes. The "need" for higher-end merchandise and affluent status symbols has quickly been replaced by a need to "circle the wagons", find value in every activity, and focus more on conserving resources as well as a greater focus on the value of the family unit interaction. The ability of retailers to adjust to these changes quickly becomes increasingly relevant. The primary product being offered by those retailers we will analyze is a food offering, which is still non-discretionary and tends to take precedence over other purchases.

According to Planet Retail, the following are strategic adjustments being seen in the current retail environment:

- ➢ Most retailers have responded to the downturn economic situation by:
  - ○ Promoting value through the expansion of discount stores, economy ranges, price investments, and increased promotions.
  - ○ Reducing costs and preserving cash by slowing down expansion plans and focusing on the most profitable stores and customer segments.
- ➢ In the next five years, the top grocery chains are expected to grow at an average compounded annual growth rate (CAGR) of 5.2 percent versus 10.8 percent in the last five years.
- ➢ The discount channel is seen as a growth format for the next five years. Led by retailers like Aldi and the Schwarz Group (Germany), the discount

channel is expected to add US$ 71 billion dollars; which is a 6.3 percent increase.

> "Proximity retailing" is the new term for small-box stores which require less capital to build and operate. Stores less than two thousand five hundred square meters will grow by 4.1 percent in the next five years, while supercenters and hypermarkets will only grow by 2.2 percent. The closer proximity addresses the future demographic changes of more single households, lower incomes, and less car ownership.

> Cash and carry and club strategies are mixed in their success. Cash and carries are a primary growth vehicle in India (with Wal-Mart and Tesco entering this year), and Russia (with the retailer Rewe). The downside of this format is the dependency upon "big ticket" general merchandise sales, and the fact that the economic downturn has stalled consumer demand for these types of purchases.

> Supercenters and hypermarkets will find a more attractive retail setting in Asia and Latin America, where the retail market is not as mature as Western Europe and North America.

> Diversified formats are still the norm, rather than exception. The ability to operate multiple formats allows for a type of "catering" to the local market. Over 80 percent of the top thirty global retailers trade in more than one channel. Over 30 percent of the top thirty retailers operate a hypermarket or supercenter format.

> Strategically, retailers that do not have a dominant format (over 75 percent of sales) are more focused on growth outside their home markets. The average of the top thirty global retailers is that they tend to generate 32 percent of sales outside of their home market.

> Western European retailers Metro, Aldi, Tesco, and Casino will return 72 percent, 62 percent, 40 percent, and 48 percent of their sales, respectively, outside of their home market in the future.

> Carrefour has been espousing the "multi-channel, single brand" strategy, which has them operating in various channel formats but using the Carrefour name for all formats. Wal-Mart also most recently added the name Wal-Mart to its smaller format.

> Central Europe and Eastern Europe will see the highest growth rates in number of outlets in the top thirty retailers. In this region, store numbers are expected to grow at a compounded annual growth rate of 11.1 percent in the future. Discounters will add the lion's share of outlets, adding two thousand one hundred stores in the next five years.

Central and Eastern Europe (CEE) will be a very attractive location for the growth of Tesco, Carrefour, Metro, Schwarz Group, and Auchan.

> Asia, long-term, is still the primary growth area for the top global retailers. Wal-Mart, Carrefour, and Tesco are continuously expanding in China (the only market where the three compete with each other), along with India. India and China have been experiencing rising property prices, food price inflation, and increased competition. Nonetheless, the potential combination of a growing middle class, an under-served market, and a burgeoning population, is too large to ignore. The global retailers are expected to add six thousand three hundred stores in the region in the next five years.

> Electronics, entertainment, and office sectors have been hit especially hard by the economic downturn. Consumers have looked at these purchases as being able to be pushed off until the economic environment settles or improves.

> Spending on home white goods has also contracted severely, due to the housing implosion in the United States, other parts of North America, and Western Europe. If a retailer does not have the diversification of Wal-Mart or Tesco, which both sell white goods, plus food, plus entertainment, then financial trouble has hit the operating cash line significantly.

> The bright spot for electronics has been the fact that more customers are choosing to stay home and not go on vacations. The term "staycation", defined as staying home for vacation and entertaining the family, has led to a slight increase in affordable and durable electronics like computer games.

> The contraction and insolvency of many small businesses has led to a downturn by office supply companies. Most office supply companies, like Staples and Office Depot, were driving their growth by infiltrating small businesses for their supply businesses. As those companies have fallen upon hard times, so have their suppliers.[32]

As a market evolves, the following normally happens:

> The under-developed market relies upon independent and "mom and pop" stores.

> With economic growth, the larger retailers enter the market with the "cash and carry" format.

- Consolidation occurs, and the large chain stores enter and form a solid operating base.
- Saturation occurs and small-box retail formats become the strategy to meet the smaller local markets and more pin-pointed customer bases.
- Legislation occurs to limit monopolies and format proliferation occurs.
- If legislation is strong enough, fragmentation ensues and the cycle begins again.
- If the legislation keeps the operating environment in its current place, then fragmentation does not occur to a major extent, but multiple formats continue to evolve.[33]

The top thirty retailer's percent of sales by channel is as follows:

Top Thirty Grocery Retailers Percent of Sales by Channel

	Convenience	Discount	Drug	Hyper	Super	Club	Other
Wal-Mart				84	1	13	1
Carrefour	2	9		59	28	2	1
Tesco	4			85	8		4
Metro				16	3	47	34
Kroger	3			97			
Schwarz		71		29			
Costco						100	
Seven&I	59			19	3		19
Target				97			3
Aldi		93			7		
Ahold	1	3	1	50	43		1
Auchan				77	21		1
Walgreens			100				
AEON	5	1	8	42	20		25
Rewe		19	1	5	44	9	22
Casino	7	7		39	33		14
Sears				25			75
Edeka		14		29	45	4	8
CVS			100				
Safeway				100			
Leclerc				90	7		4
Supervalu		11		88	1		
Woolwrth	12			8	67		12
Sainsbury	2			87	7		3
ITM		4			87	7	3
Coles	15			10	43		32
Morrisons				81	19		
Delhaize	2			69	28	1	1
Rite Aid			100				
Loblaw				61	20	4	16

Source: Planet Retail, 2009

It is interesting to note that North American retailers, due to economies of scale and the ability for "singular format only" retailers (like CVS and Walgreen's) to be successful, primarily trade in one format and one channel. Western European and other international retailers are more land-locked and must operate in multiple channels to grow.

Tesco has been able to successfully use its brand throughout multiple formats and channels. Now, Carrefour and Wal-Mart are joining the mix of retailers attempting to do the same.[34] When a brand has enough positive equity with consumers, it can transfer this brand equity from format to format. In the case of Carrefour, the company is converting its Champion grocery stores to the Carrefour Market banner. Additionally, all of its smaller, neighborhood stores (Shopi, 8 a Huit, Marche Plus, Proxi, and Sherpa) are being re-branded as Carrefour City in urban areas and Carrefour Contact in rural areas.[35] Wal-Mart has recently added the words "Walmart" to its smaller format. By using a common brand, the synergies of advertising and brand recognition grow exponentially. Sainsbury's and Casino, two other Western European retailers, are also using the same concept.

Hypermarkets and supercenters: In the formats of hypermarkets and supercenters, the growth has slowed some in the developed areas (North America and Western Europe), but the format is the preferred growth model for Asia, Central and Eastern Europe, Africa, and the Middle East. In the Middle East and Africa, the number of hypermarkets is predicted to double by the year 2014. This expansion is mostly fueled by the French retailers Carrefour and Casino.[36] The format's attractiveness is fueled by the ability to offer a one-stop shopping experience and offer the option to consolidate logistical deliveries across geographies. The potential issues with hypermarkets include: fresh and foodservice attractiveness, large square footage to cover fixed expenses when sales are slow, and the discretionary aspect of the non-foods carried in these stores.

China is a primary target for most international retailers. Tesco, Wal-Mart, and Carrefour compete head to head in China, along with the likes of Auchan, Seven & I, AEON, and Casino. Most retailers have used the hypermarket format, with growth increasing five-fold in the last four years. In China, the top thirty grocers represent six hundred five hypermarkets and superstores, compared to only one-hundred twenty-five in 2003. In the next five years,

China expects to add an additional five-hundred thirty-five hypermarkets, making the total one-thousand one-hundred forty.[37]

Carrefour is the leader in China currently, namely because the retailer adapted its format to local tastes immediately upon entering the country. In China, the hypermarkets tend to be located in the middle of the cities, rather than the outskirts (like in North America and Western Europe). This proximity to the population causes hypermarkets to be visited two to three times per day by customers, which is not the norm in other parts of the world. Chinese customers usually bike or walk to the stores, which limits their ability to carry large amounts of products home with them. The primary deciding factor for selecting where to shop usually lies in the retailer's ability to offer the freshest and widest array of produce.[38]

Supermarkets and neighborhood stores: Growth of the smaller supermarkets and neighborhood stores will be the highest in North America. Tesco's entry into the United States spurred growth of alternate formats by Wal-Mart, Supervalu, and Safeway. Growth of the supermarket and neighborhood store format in the Middle East and Africa will almost solely be driven by Casino. Casino is the only top thirty operator with a significant presence in the region, especially Sub-Saharan Africa. Casino competes against Shoprite and Pick n Pay in this geography. In Central and Eastern Europe, the supermarket format growth will be primarily driven by Rewe in Russia. Rewe's Billa banner will see growth in Bulgaria, Croatia, Czech Republic, Poland, and Romania. Tesco will lead the expansion in Central Europe and Carrefour will lead the growth in Greece, Poland, and Romania. The supermarket format in Latin America will be driven by Wal-Mart's acquisition of Chilean retailer D&S. Asia and Oceania growth in Australia, Japan, and South Korea will be more controlled.[39]

Wal-Mart's Neighborhood Market format, a direct response to Tesco's Fresh and Easy format, was designed to be fresh-focused and value-driven. Neighborhood Market's aim is to be more focused on full-service grocery, an in-store kitchen, a bakery, deli, and full-service checkouts. Wal-Mart's Neighborhood Market focuses on national brands, while Tesco's Fresh and Easy's sales were made up of 70 percent store brands. Neighborhood Markets's pricing is not comparable to a regular Wal-Mart store, since it reflects the increased costs of fresh in-store foods; but they are still competitively priced on the staples of bread, milk, butter, bananas, and eggs.

In late 2008, Woolworth's launched a new fresh-focused format in Australia. These stores, named Thomas Dux, are approximately five-hundred square meters, half of which is focused on fresh meat, fruit, dairy, bread, and an extended dairy. There are three thousand items in the grocery assortment, and the format is designed to be the opposite of a "normal" Woolworth's store. The feel is supposed to be "homey", with the staff sampling the fruit themselves, warm lighting, and merchandising in a "product first" mentality.

Discount stores: The discount store format is based upon a limited range of products sold in smaller stores. These stores are resistant to, if not helped by, recessionary times. As the economy has worsened, the discount store format has gained in popularity. Discount stores dominate the Western Europe landscape. Where they number in the thousands in the rest of the world's operating areas (two thousand in the United States), discount stores number around twenty-five thousand in Western Europe, and are expected to grow by another nine thousand in Western Europe alone by 2014. Central and Eastern Europe are also growing at a quicker rate (14 percent) than the rest of the world. Europe is the "home turf" for discount stores, being led by Aldi and Schwarz Group's Lidl. In 2008, Lidl had more stores than Aldi in Western Europe for the first time ever (although Aldi still had a larger sales turnover). The third ranking operator of discount stores in Europe is Carrefour, which runs their discount stores under the banners of Ed, Dia, and Minipreco. The fourth largest operator is Edeka, which operates Netto and recently acquired Plus from Tengelmann.

With Western Europe already having high penetration of the discount format, the large growth of the format is going to come from the United Kingdom, Ireland, Spain, Portugal, and Switzerland. Germany, the leader in this format with eleven thousand stores, still expects the number to climb to fifteen thousand in the next five years, as Aldi is attacked by Lidl, Edeka's Netto, and Rewe Group's Penny. Central and Eastern Europe will see the natural geographical expansion of the format, fueled by Schwarz's Lidl, Rewe Group's Penny, Aldi, Carrefour, Ahold, Casino, Auchan, and Delhaize Group. Central and Eastern Europe were hit extremely hard by the economic downturn, and are the most receptive to this format.

North America is certainly also regarded as fertile ground for the advancement of the discount format. A format focusing on smaller sized stores, lower costs, lower prices, and ease of shopping is poised to do well in an economic slump inside the United States. The major obstacle faced by the discount format is the fact that they have not been widely accepted by Americans. The American public is relatively spoiled by the vast array of products available inside grocery stores, coupled with great service. The discount format is limited assortment and low service. Also fighting the discount store advance is the fact that most of the world's largest brands were formed in the United States. The discount format, as we know it today, is focused on chain-specific store brands or "off brands". Store brand acceptance is not nearly as wide in the United States as it is in the rest of the world. In fact, it has taken Aldi more than thirty years to top the one thousand store mark in the United States.

Aldi's primary discount store competitor is Save a Lot. But, Save a Lot has conservative growth projected, while Aldi expects to open one-hundred stores per year. The discount format which is focused upon dollar stores is showing tremendous growth, though. These stores, led by Dollar General, Family Dollar Stores, and Dollar Tree, number in the five thousand to twenty thousand stores each. As these stores expand their food offerings, the increased traffic multiplied by the sheer number of stores, makes this format a venerable competitor.

Internationally, the discount store format is supported by the likes of Wal-Mart and Carrefour, with three-hundred fifty-seven and seven-hundred thirty-seven stores each, respectively. Carrefour's Dia stores are found in Argentina and Brazil, while Wal-Mart's D&S and Sam's have been focusing on other parts of Latin America. Casino also operates over one-hundred stores in Latin America. In Asia and Oceania, discount stores are expected to see growth in the 8 percent range, the second highest outside of Europe and much faster than North America. Carrefour is leading this expansion, with a strong presence in Turkey and China. AEON and Aldi are also very strong in the Asia and Oceania region; Aldi in Australia and AEON in Japan.

The discount format is well-received in Asia and Oceania, and growth will continue at a rapid pace. Aldi expects to double its store numbers in the next five years. The overall leader in this region, though, is Turkish discount operator BIM with over two thousand two-hundred stores in the region. The second largest network is run by LAWSON in Japan. In Africa and the Middle East, there is very little growth in the discount format expected in the next five years. Only Casino operates in the area, and it is only a handful of stores. Shoprite operates over one hundred stores in South African markets, GSL is showing strong growth in Saudi Arabia, and BIM is expected to enter Morocco in 2009.

Cash and carries and warehouse clubs: The format of cash and carries and warehouse clubs is a high growth format in Asia and Oceania. These stores primarily focus on supplying the large number of independent stores, serving as their supplier and warehouse. The number of cash and carries operated by the top thirty is expected to double in Asia and Oceania in the next five years. The world's largest cash and carry operator is Metro. Metro was one of the first retailers to enter India, and is expanding into Pakistan and Kazakhstan. The future growth will be driven by Wal-Mart, Tesco, Carrefour, and Costco. The Middle Eastern and African region is also set to experience heavy growth, primarily spurred by Metro's entry into Egypt in 2009.

In Central and Eastern Europe, growth will be driven by Metro. This growth will be seen heavily in Russia, Poland, and the Ukraine. Western Europe is not as fertile for the expansion of cash and carries, as the available land is scarce. Expansion will be seen by Metro and Rewe, with the potential that Costco will enter the Irish market in the near future. Brazil and Mexico are prime expansion spots for cash and carries, driven by Wal-Mart's Maxxi Atacado chain in Brazil, Casino's Assai chain in Brazil, and Wal-Mart's Sam's Club and Costco in Mexico. The North American market is the home to the most warehouse clubs, with over one thousand one-hundred. Wal-Mart's Sam's Club has the most number of stores (six hundred), but Costco leads the market in sales turnover.

Costco has just recently entered the Australian market, with its first store in Melbourne's Docklands. The Dockland's outlet was chosen due to its proximity to small and medium businesses, growing population, and close distance to freeways and public transportation. The store sizes in Australia will range from thirteen thousand to fourteen thousand square meters. Approximately 40 percent of the floor space is dedicated to food, with the rest allocated to general merchandise.

Convenience and forecourt formats: The convenience and forecourt formats are expected to grow by 3.4 percent in the next five years. Central and Eastern Europe are set for the highest growth rate, albeit from a small base, due to the expansion of Tesco's adding new convenience stores in the Czech Republic and Hungary. The growth in Poland will come from Carrefour's chain launched in 2007 called 5 Minut. Through the Latin American region, Brazil and Colombia will see the most growth from the top thirty grocers. Growth will be in the 6.6 percent range, fueled by Carrefour and Casino's Carrefour Express and Extra Facil stores, respectively.

In Western Europe, Asia, and North America, retailers use convenience stores to fill in gaps that cannot be satisfied by other formats. These formats also offer the ability to hone their skills in ready to eat meals and top-up (or fill-in) shopping. Seven and I dominates North America and Asia with the 7-Eleven brand. Throughout Asia, Tesco will be driving growth with its convenience stores in China, Japan, South Korea, Thailand, and Turkey. Most stores attempt to coordinate their food and other assorted goods with offering gasoline. The convenience store format is not expected to see much growth in Africa and the Middle East.

Casino is looking to expand from its current base, and has identified the convenience store format as a desirable growth engine. The convenience format for Casino is represented by the banners Petit Casino, SPAR, Vival, and Monop. In early 2009, Casino announced the launching of Chez Jean. This partnership with Relay is a hybrid between a coffee shop and a grocery store. The assortment includes coffee, groceries, fresh bread, flowers, newspapers, tickets and lottery tickets. The format also offers foodservice, Wi-Fi, mobile recharging stations, and clean restrooms. The total selling area equates to three-hundred eighty square meters.

The Chez Jean stores offer foodservice based upon the time of day. In the morning, the service counter is called "Reveil" (wake up), offering bakery items and coffee. During lunch time, the same counter switches to "Ca gargouille" (rumbling tummy), and sells sandwiches, desserts, and beverages. During the dinner hours, the counter switches to "SOS frigo vide" (SOS empty fridge), and offers salads, cooked meals, and desserts. Groceries are supplied by Casino, and offer a much more consolidated assortment than regular convenience stores. The grocery offering includes yogurts, frozen foods, mineral water, biscuits, wines, champagne, fruit, sushi, and beauty products. Surrounding this assortment, there is an offering of newspapers, magazines, and novels.

Drugstore and pharmacy formats: The drugstore and pharmacy channel will have a much slower expansion than other channels in the next five years. The channel is not a priority for most of the top thirty grocers. There is very little internationalization of drugstore and pharmacy retailers. AEON's Welcia only operates in Japan. Walgreens, CVS, and Rite Aid operate primarily in North America. Walgreens and Boots formed an alliance in 2014, which is one of the first major steps into a globalized platform for pharmacy and drug stores. Although store count growth will be slow, the sales growth should be brisk. The aging population, addition and expansion of grocery assortment, and the new freedom of some of the pharmacy markets in Germany and Scandinavia, should help this format grow at over 2 percent in the next five years. The fact that the channel is relatively insulated from the economic downturn, due to the non-discretionary aspect of what it sells, should help maintain and encourage growth.

Fueling growth internationally will be AEON's Welcia network of stores, accounting for all the drugstores and pharmacies in Asia and Oceania from top thirty grocers; and Australia's Woolworth's, rumored to be looking to acquire Australian Pharmaceutical Industries (operating five-hundred drugstores and pharmacies in Australia).

In North America, Walgreens, CVS, and Rite Aid continue their decent store number expansions. Walgreens alone plans to open five-hundred net new stores in the next five years, in addition to growing its alliance platform with Boots. CVS most recently acquired the five-hundred store Long's Drugs chain and has opened a new format called Beauty 360.

With a revised pharmaceutical law enacted in Japan in 2009, AEON's expansion will be centered upon drugstores and pharmacies in the country. The pressure for health care reform and the increased promotion of self-medication, will drive the drugstore format. To expand, AEON has taken minority stakes in regional drugstore chains like CFS. Welcia now has a drugstore alliance of more than one thousand seven-hundred stores, coming from nine regional drug chains.[40]

Wal-Mart plans to offer four-hundred in-store health clinics in the next five years. There are currently thirty-six locations, using "The Clinic at Walmart" as the brand. The first clinics opened in April, 2008 in Atlanta, and they are co-branded with local hospitals. The average visit costs a customer from $50 to $65.[41]

Each of these formats described above has positive and negative aspects to their development, primarily focused upon each of the various global challenges that differ by region. Where new small-box supermarket formats are driving the competition versus convenience stores, improvements in their fresh offerings are making the convenience format stronger. As drugstores are relatively recession-resistant, so are the dollar stores, which are selling the same non-drug items as the pharmacies. And, as hypermarkets are the strongest growth format in Asia and Oceania, they are relatively stable in North America. Each of the major top thirty chains is using the multi-format approach to be able to ensure they have a response for whichever market they would like to enter and whether or not the economy is improving or disintegrating. Land, and its scarcity or propensity, is a key variable in deciding upon the appropriate formats to use by country. As well, the government always plays a role in whether or not the economics inside the country are ripe for retail growth or are limited by governmental factors.

The importance of being able to cater to the local needs and nuances cannot be passed over by any of the major retailers. An inner-city retail shopping experience in Japan is going to differ greatly from an inner-city experience in Detroit. The fresh food offering in a convenience format in Copenhagen will differ greatly from the local customer needs for food service in Moscow. On top of that, the needs of the customers in the morning will differ from the needs at lunch, or at dinner, or at midnight. The strong retailers understand these unique variables in operating globally, and offer the multi-tier formats to remain strong.

The strategic designs of each of the global retailers centers very closely to the same operating methods as the global consumer good companies. Localization is the key to success, with multiple formats used as the answer to convey a brand image to as many customers as possible, while still fitting the store format into the desired locations.

Key Findings:

- The economic malaise showed the validity in offering a diverse array of products through a variation of formats. As one format suffers, the other shows an upswing. This type of diversification is an important element in global retailing.

- In the next five years, the top grocery chains are expected to grow at a compounded annual growth rate (CAGR) of 5.2 percent versus the robust growth of 10.8 percent the last five years.

- The discount channel is seen as the highest growth format for the next five years, led by retailers like Aldi and the Schwarz Group. The discount channel is expected to add US$ 71 billion in the next five years, which is a 6.3 percent increase in sales.

- "Proximity retailing" is the newest term for small-box stores which require less capital to build and operate. Stores with less than two thousand five-hundred square feet will grow by 4.1 percent in the next five years, compared to supercenter and hypermarket growth of 2.2 percent.

- Cash and carry formats are the primary growth vehicle in emerging countries like India. Supercenters and hypermarkets will see stronger growth in Asia and Latin America, where the geography is more fertile for one-stop shopping and the format proliferation has not happened as it has in the United States or the United Kingdom.

- Asia is the primary growth area for most global retailers, with Tesco, Carrefour, and Wal-Mart competing head to head in China. Carrefour is currently the market leader in China.

- Market evolution is important in understanding which format to bring to which countries. Under-developed markets rely upon independent and "mom and pop" stores.

- As they evolve, larger retailers enter the marketplace with large chain stores and "cash and carries." As saturation occurs, the smaller format becomes preferred and has another growth spurt. As the market evolves even more, multiple formats are developed and become more of a primary strategy for the larger retailers.

- Most retailers in the top thirty operate multiple formats, with Ahold and Rewe operating a store in almost every format available (convenience, discount, drug, hypermarket, supermarket, club, and other).

- North American retailers tend to trade heavily in one format, while European retailers have perfected the ability to trade in multiple formats. Tesco and Carrefour have been successful in using their brand name in each format, to allow for brand equity to move from one format to another.

➢ Hypermarkets and supercenters will slow in growth in North America, but are the preferred format for growth in Asia, Central and Eastern Europe, Africa, and the Middle East. The format's attractiveness is fueled by the ability to offer a one-stop shopping experience and offer the ability to consolidate logistical deliveries across geographies.

➢ Supermarkets and neighborhood stores will grow the most in North America, where supercenters have proliferated the marketplace. Tesco's Fresh and Easy and Wal-Mart's Marketside and Neighborhood Stores are poised for explosive growth in the United States. This format allows larger retailers the ability to reach customers in smaller marketing areas and with a differentiated assortment.

➢ Discount stores, which are resistant and even aided by economic downturns, dominate the Western European landscape. Western Europe will also be the primary area for growth of this format. Germany is the leader in this format with eleven thousand stores, currently. This format has not caught on well in the United States, where the lack of assortment, the lack of excitement, and the need to bag your own groceries, do not make visiting these stores pleasant for Americans.

➢ Cash and carries are a high growth format in Asia and Oceania. These stores are primarily focused on supplying smaller independent stores. The number of cash and carries is expected to double in Asia and Oceania in the next five years. The world's largest cash and carry operator is Metro, which was the first foreign retailer to enter India. As Metro enters the Middle east and Africa, this format is set for explosive growth. Russia, Poland, and the Ukraine will also share in this growth.

➢ Convenience and forecourt formats are only expected to grow by 3.4 percent in the next five years. The highest region for growth rate will be Central and Eastern Europe. Latin America, Brazil, and Colombia will see the most growth from the top thirty retailers.

➢ Drugstore and pharmacy formats will not have as high a rate of expansion, mostly due to the fact that this format does not cross borders very well at all. The drug laws and regulations make global expansion almost impossible.

Discussion Questions

1. Name the growth formats of retail for the next five years, and why they are growing.

2. Name the growth regions of retail for the next five years, and why they are growing.

3. Is it better to offer "one size fits all" retail formats or smaller, more specialized formats in the United States? In India? Explain your response.

4. How accepted are store brands in the United States? England? Why the difference?

5. To a retailer what are the pro's and cons of a strong store brand program?

6. Name a store you have visited in another country, and the difference between that store and what you "expected to see". Explain why they were different.

7. You are starting a new food retailer, with headquarters in Dallas, Texas. Describe that retailer in terms of formats, commodities offered, geographical considerations, size, logistics, etc. Be detailed in your response.

8. What changes have you made in the last five years to your spending activity? What factors have impacted your behaviors?

Case One- Nestle SA

Nestle SA, located in Vevey, Switzerland, is the largest food manufacturing company in the world. With 283,000 associates, Nestle produces revenue of US$ 109.9 billion per year and net profit of US$ 18.04 billion.[42] Nestlé's most recent results show an organic growth of 3.5 percent (versus a 5 percent projection), and a thirty basis points improvement on its margin before interest and tax.

The company was formed in 1867, when two Swiss enterprises were joined to become Nestle. In August, 1867, Charles and George Page, from the United States, established the Anglo-Swiss Condensed Milk Company in Cham. In September of the same year, Henri Nestle, from Switzerland, developed a milk-based baby food and began to sell it. Over the next thirty years, the two companies began to offer similar products and were bitter rivals in the marketplace. By 1905, the two companies merged to become the Nestle and Anglo-Swiss Condensed Milk Company. This name was the proper name until 1947, when the name was changed to Nestle Alimentana SA after the company purchased Maggi. The company's current name was adopted in 1977.[43]

Through multiple World Wars, Nestle added and developed new products, in the lines of chocolate and Nescafe, while continuing to build plants throughout the world. Added to the line-up were Crosse and Blackwell in 1950, Findus in 1963, Libby's in 1971, Stouffer's in 1973, a shareholding in L'Oreal in 1974, and Alcon Laboratories in 1977. As the company continued its growth, it was able to add Carnation in 1984, and Rowntree Mackintosh in 1988 (including the Willy Wonka brand). San Pellegrino was added in 1997, Spillers Petfoods in 1998, Ralston Purina in 2002, Dreyer's Ice Cream and Chef America (creator of Hot Pockets) also in 2002, and then added the Jenny Craig brand. In 2005, Nestle purchased the Greek company Delta Ice Cream, which made Nestle the world's largest ice cream maker with a 17.5 percent share of the world's ice cream sales.[44]

By 2007, Nestle had added the Medical nutrition division of Novartis Pharmaceutical, Ovaltine, Gerber, and a partnership with Belgian chocolate maker Pierre Marcolini.[45]

In the categories where Nestle operates, one researched study showed growth potential, by value and volume, for five food categories: bakery and cereals, chilled food, confectionary, frozen food, and sweet and savory snacks. Here are the results of the study:

> **Asia- Pacific:** In the Asia-Pacific, the bakery segment showed the strongest potential for growth, with the high year's being 2013 and annual growth around 2.3 percent. Chilled foods will have annual growth rates of .8 percent, but will have a strong base of sales to maintain.

> **Eastern Europe:** In Eastern Europe, chilled foods will have annual growth of 11.7 percent, and confectionary will have a lower annual growth rate at 6.7 percent.

> **North America:** North American growth will be driven by frozen food at 2.6 percent, but bakery is the largest category in annual revenue.

> **Western Europe:** Chilled food will spur the growth in Western Europe, with annual growth at 4.1 percent. Frozen food growth will be below average, at 1.1 percent.

> **Latin America:** As an emerging economic area of the world, all categories will experience exceptionally high growth rates.[46]

In only five categories, the growth and selling strategies and tactics are going to differ drastically by geographical marketplace. Primary drivers of growth differentiation being emerging market status, health and wellness focus, industrial growth, and commodity fluctuations. According to the Roper Report Worldwide Power Brands study, Nestle is the fourth most recognizable brand in the world.[47]

Nestle SA operates over 480 factories in 86 countries. With 283,000 employees, the cultural diversity is immense. The factories are broken out in this manner:

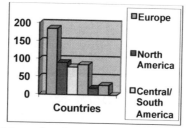

Figure 5.1 Nestle SA Factories by Continent
Source: The Nestle Creating Shared Value Report (Nestle Public Affairs, 2008)

Nestlé's employee spread is 38.3 percent in the Americas, 34.5 percent in Europe, and 27.2 percent in Asia, Oceania, and Africa. Sales and growth are represented in the following manner:

Nestle Sales and Organic Growth by Product Category

Product category	Sales (CHF billion)	Organic growth
Powdered/ liquid beverages	$17.9	10.3%
Nestle Waters	$10.4	6.6%
Milk products/ ice cream	$20.7	7.8%
Nestle Nutrition	$8.4	9.7%
Prepared dishes	$18.5	4.0%
Confectionary	$12.3	5.3%
Pet Care	$12.1	7.0%
Pharmaceutical	$7.3	11.0%
Total	$107.5	

Source: The Nestle Creating Shared Value Report

Some of the global highlights from the product categories:

> Nestle is the world's largest milk company, sourcing 11.8 million tons of milk from more than thirty countries. Nestlé's approach includes the development of milk districts, which involves regular purchasing of milk from local farmers, regardless of how much or how little they produce.
> Nestle purchased 750,000 tons of green coffee in 2006, with about 13 percent of it coming directly from farmers, making Nestle the world's largest direct purchaser of coffee.
> Only about 2 percent of the world's specialty grade coffees meet the specific profile of Nespresso Grands Crus. In 2003, Nespresso added an additional "A" to its "AA" standards. This additional "A" incorporated sustainability into its grading system.
> Nestle Nutrition is a global, standalone business that delivers science-based nutrition products in the following categories: infant nutrition, healthcare nutrition, performance nutrition, and weight management.
> In 2007, Nestle reached over 10 million people through its Nestle education programs and initiatives.[48]

At over US$ 100 billion in revenue annually, Nestle SA is a venerable food manufacturing institution. Carrying lines like Kit Kat, Nescafe, Friskies, Nespresso, and Maggi, Nestle SA is a true example of a global, multi-national brand powerhouse.[49] Nestle SA's portfolio consists of 8,000 brands, 29 which have sales over US$ 1 billion, with 1.2 billion of its products sold each day.[50] Only 20 percent of its sales are through the ten largest retailers in the world-including Wal-Mart and Tesco.[51] In order to attain global synergies, while attracting the local customer, Nestle SA has formed multiple guidelines, which all business units must follow.

These guidelines are as follows:

> Nestlé SA's business objective is to manufacture and market the company's products in such a way as to create value that can be sustained over the long term for shareholders, employees, consumers, and business partners.

> Nestlé SA does not favor short-term profit at the expense of successful long-term business development.

> Nestlé SA recognizes that its consumers have a sincere and legitimate interest in the behavior, beliefs and actions of the company behind brands in which they place their trust, and that without its consumers the company would not exist.

> Nestlé SA believes that, as a general rule, legislation is the most effective safeguard of responsible conduct, although in certain areas, additional guidance to staff in the form of voluntary business principles is beneficial in order to ensure that the highest standards are met throughout the organization.

> Nestlé SA is conscious of the fact that the success of a corporation is a reflection of the professionalism, conduct and the responsible attitude of its management and employees. Therefore recruitment of the right people and ongoing training and development are crucial.

> Nestlé SA continues to maintain its commitment to follow and respect all applicable local laws in each of its markets.[52]

By setting applicable guidelines, the brand essence of Nestle can be maintained no matter the operating country.

Before applying a local strategy to marketing of its products, Nestle SA established guidelines for its environmental footprint as well as social accountability. In the document, The Nestle Creating Shared Report, Nestle provides a detailed doctrine for all operating countries and brands to follow. It is important to note that the umbrella company philosophy needed to be established before any localized strategies could be developed.

Nestle SA's global product marketing strategy can best be described as a hybrid; where some of the brands are global and some of the brands are local. But, in all cases, the local taste preferences must be met for each product. Petraea Heynike, head of Nestle SA's Chocolate, Biscuits, and Confectionery, described the Nestle confection approach as "local, local, local. We have different brands in our 61 markets, and that is our strength. 70 percent of our sales are with local brands, with only Kit Kat and Nestle as our global brands.".[53]

Of course, localized brands are not without peril. In 2007, Nestle SA's chief executive officer discovered that Nestle SA was producing 130,000 variations of its brands, and 30 percent were not making any money. Nestle SA has implemented new SAP software, called Globe - Global Business Excellence. For example, this software determines how much raw cocoa Nestle SA factories use and how many Nestle Crunch bars are produced.[54] In this manner, Nestle SA is able to gain global synergies and local appeal. In order to achieve this goal, Nestle SA has broken the world into three geographic zones: Zone Europe, Zone Americas, and Zone Oceania and Africa.[55]

A few global product highlights from the Nestle Management Report:

> Over 90 percent of the Nestle products sold in China are made in China. The Nestle Research and Design center in Shanghai uses local insight, including knowledge of Chinese functional ingredients, to help ensure that product formulations meet the needs of families for high quality, enjoyable and tasty foods which provide the appropriate nutrition at an affordable price.
> Making nutritious foods available and accessible to everyone, everywhere as a primary mission, Nestle initiated a program called "Popularly Positioned Products (PPP)"; which brings the best quality, highly nutritious foods and beverages within reach of billions of people at the "base of the pyramid". Their incomes are comparatively low, yet sufficient to provide spending power on trusted products that contribute to improving their quality of life.
> Accessibility means affordable low prices and taking our products to where consumers live. In various markets, Nestle sells products in street kiosks, from mobile vending carts, or "door-to-door". Nestlé's "PPP" sales are growing profitably at an annual rate of 27 percent.

- Thirty percent of the world's population is anemic, and 35 percent have insufficient iodine in their diet. Nestle adds low-cost micronutrients in the form of vitamins, minerals, and trace elements, to address the most prevalent deficiencies at affordable prices. One such example is the Bear Brand in the Philippines, which is a low-cost alternative providing vital proteins in soya, dhai, and cereals.

- In Central and West Africa, 65 million Maggi bouillon cubes are sold every day. For affordability, they are sold individually at extremely low cost. They are widely distributed in neighborhood stores and by local women. Maggi bouillon cubes achieve a 45 percent household penetration in rural areas, and address micronutrient deficiencies such as iodine.

- Nestle principles concerning appropriate communication with consumers have been part of the Nestle Corporate Business Principles since they were first published in 1999, and are required reading for all marketing staff and advertising agencies globally. These principles include specific criteria for communication with children, aimed at encouraging moderation, healthy dietary habits and physical activity, not undermining the authority of parents or creating unrealistic expectations of popularity or success.

- Nestle has thirty-one brands that return an annual turnover exceeding US$ 1 billion in sales. Many brands are multi-billion sales brands, such as Nescafe, Purina, Maggi, and Gerber. Nestle water encompasses seventy-two brands world-wide. Over four thousand cups of Nescafe are consumed every second. Globally, Nescafe owns 23 percent of the world's total coffee category.

- Nescafe launched Nescafe Protect in Mexico and many Asian countries, as a "good for you" coffee solution. As described by Nestle, Nescafe Protect has a superb, mild and smooth taste; but also includes beans processed through a proprietary process that preserves the cholorogenic acids and polyphenols to give it three times more antioxidants than green tea.

- In Malaysia, Milo is the "national drink for children", where it sells considerably more than any soft drink. Nestle uses proprietary technology in the malt process that improves the carbohydrate mix which, together with Actigen-E, optimizes energy release.

- Contrex is a French mineral water naturally rich in calcium, helping bone structure and its upkeep. Since 1954, it has been the favorite of

France's weight-conscious women and is now sold in more than forty countries.

➢ In Chile, Nestle sells "60 percent milk" take-home ice cream, which gives stronger nutritional values and the pleasure of creamier taste.

➢ In South Africa, Nestle sells Nestle Pure Life water from street kiosks, which also act as supply points for neighborhood vendors, ensuring safe healthy water along with creating local jobs.

➢ In over fifty countries across Europe, Asia, and Latin America, Nestle sells Nestle Fitness cereal brand which is a 99 percent fat-free cereal where one serving provides 50 percent of the recommended daily allowance of eight vitamins and 20 percent of the recommended daily allowance of iron.[56]

As a global company, and with over 280,000 associates, issues can erupt from all areas of the world. Here are a few examples of issues Nestle has dealt with in various parts of the world:

➢ Nestle was highly criticized for promoting processed cow's milk (its baby formula) as a better substitute for breast-feeding. In economically dis-advantage countries, this practice was seen as mis-leading and un-warranted. Public outcry led to a boycott of Nestle baby milk in 1977, which is still in effect today. Nestle agreed to abide by the International Code of Marketing of Breast-milk Substitutes in 2004, established by the World Health Organization. In fact, as the largest food manufacturing company in the world, Nestle is also the most boycotted company in the world.[57]

➢ In 2002, Nestle brought on negative publicity when it demanded US$ 6 million in payment from Ethiopia, one of the world's poorest countries. Twenty years earlier, the Ethiopian government had seized a Nestle subsidiary and made it its own company. The eventual offer of settlement from Ethiopia, and the payment received by Nestle caused an uproar in inequities, and led to Nestlé's donating the money to famine relief projects in the area.[58]

➢ In 2005, Nestle was accused of selling tons of contaminated animal feed in Venezuela.[59] The local brands of Dog Chow, Cat Chow, Puppy Chow, Fiel, Friskies, Gatsy, K-Nina, Nutriperro, Perrarina, and Pajarina were reportedly contaminated by a supplier who stored the corn used in the feed incorrectly, which grew a fungus with a large amount of aflatoxin.

Nestle was ordered to pay compensation to the owners of the impacted animals.[60]

➢ Bottled water has been the source of controversy for many years, including a Perrier bottling plant in Stanwood, Michigan which was heavily protested, a requested extension of five years to bottle water in Guelph, Ontario which was not granted, and a plan to open a large bottled water plant using the water from Mt. Shasta which was heavily protested.[61]

➢ In 2004, Greenpeace tests found genetically-modified organisms in Chinese Nesquik. A second test was negative. A Chinese woman sued Nestle.[62]

➢ In April, 2006, a *Forbes* article accused Nestle of buying chocolate from slave labor plantations.[63] In the article, the United Nations estimated 284,000 child laborers work on cocoa farms in West Africa, especially the Ivory Coast. As a result, Nestle signed an agreement called the Cocoa Protocol, which states that it would find a method to certify its chocolate did not come from slave labor.[64]

➢ In 2008, the Hong Kong government stated that they found melamine in Chinese-made Nestle milk products. The product was called Dairy Farm Milk. Nestle tested its products and confirmed that they were safe and melamine-free.[65]

In an interview with Bob Leonidas, President of Nestle Canada, there was a specific focus on Nestlé's international operating procedures, localization efforts, and global versus local principles. The following is a recap of the interview:

Question 1: How does your company handle the various cultural differences across borders?
Response: Nestle utilizes local market research and local employees to gain the needed local market intelligence to operate properly.

Question 2: Does your company have a specific means of sharing local values with expatriates you send to various countries?
Response: No, but we try to immerse them in the local culture. We ensure they attend research focus groups and visit consumers in their homes.

Question 3: Does your company value or participate in bringing inpatriates into the existing global management team?
Response: Yes, on our twelve person global team we have nine nationalities.

Question 4: Does your company have different strategies for emerging versus established markets?

Response: Yes, we have lower priced products for emerging markets. We are also building factories in emerging markets, and utilize different routes to market in emerging countries. For example, we may use street vendors in those markets to reach the end-user easier.

Question 5: When your company enters a country, is the ability to work with (and possibly assimilate) the existing cultures a consideration (or is the business opportunity the primary consideration)?

Response: Nestle wants to work in the local culture and country. This is the concept of Creating Shared Value, jobs, economies, etcetera.

Question 6: What steps have been implemented to communicate your existing company values into the new business office, especially if merging with an existing local office?

Response: Nestle brings in expatriates to teach the Nestle cultural principles, while also working to understand the local needs. We have written Nestle management and leadership principles.

Question 7: How do you ensure that expatriates are rewarded for their willingness to move their families to foreign countries, and what types of people fit the mold for becoming expatriates?

Response: We have extra/ special benefits, private schooling, housing allowances, generous home leave, and you receive credit years of service for your time abroad. This credit allows you to retire early, if you so wish.

In a subsequent interview, the following questions were asked of Mr. Leonidas:

> ➢ How does your company determine when a product should be locally altered or when it should maintain its consistent traits from other markets?
> ➢ In what ways has your company adapted products to emerging economies versus established economies?
> ➢ In countries with low per capita income rates, what is the main focus of the products?
> ➢ Even in low demographic markets, does your company try to address the innate aspirational needs in each consumer? After survival needs, does your company still find that teens are as connected as in established economies?
> ➢ How does your company use viral and social networking to connect with consumers?

> Have you identified "ideal customers" in your psychographic target markets that become your social spokespeople?
> What is your primary data source in determining product positioning in each country?

Bob Leonidas responded with the following responses regarding Nestlé's global branding and customer connectivity:

> Food is taste driven. For example, in chocolate, Nestle targets the Hershey palette in the United States, Canada follows the tastes from the United Kingdom. Nestle uses Nespresso for each country's taste profile.
> In lower demographic economies, Nestle uses two finger Kit Kats to lower the retail price, uses skim milk powder in Mexico, and sells Maggi Bouillon Cubes one at a time in Africa.
> In the low per capita countries, survival is the first concern, and very little attention is paid to aspirational marketing. The focus is on nutrition.
> In regards to social and viral marketing, no one has "cracked the code" for measuring sales and market share. Although it is difficult in social and viral, it is similarly difficult in television, print, and radio.
> Heavy users of each product are the key. We need to market and connect to what resonates with our most loyal consumers.
> To determine the best methods of customer connectivity and product usage, Nestle goes into customers' houses, checks pantries, monitors eating patterns, and performs kitchen walk-arounds. Nestle still has more of a need for localization in regards to taste profiles.
> As opposed to Procter and Gamble, Nestle is in the food business where the driver of sales is taste. The driver of household goods sold by Procter and Gamble is being usage-oriented. Pet food is the same taste profile throughout the world.
> We call offering the right products with low costs in low per capita areas "Popularly Positioned Products".
> In China, Nestle uses the two finger bar, does not use milk chocolate, and uses a chocolate compound coating to avoid melting.
> For Nescafe soluble coffee, Nestle uses the same trademark but different blends throughout the world. In Canada, the coffee is stronger and more robust. In the United States, the coffee is weaker and milder.

- To the contrary, Nespresso coffee capsules are one product, one profile, and is a global brand.
- Nestle will change product positioning by brand, targeting, demographics, and consumer target.
- Nestle believes in local management and local efforts.
- Nestle exists to serve the customer. We try to get into the heavy-user's mindset.[66]

Nespresso planned to see double digit sales growth, open two more production plants, and open at least one hundred eighty more boutiques. Nespresso, is currently considered by Nestle to be its hottest brand. It offers portioned coffee products that replicate a café-style brew at home with coffee in capsules for machines that brew one cup at a time. At an average yearly growth of over thirty percent, the popularity of the brand continues to expand. As a truly global brand, Nespresso is expecting growth in established markets like Germany and France, along with other emerging countries and the United States. Currently, ninety percent of sales are in Europe, with only five percent in the Americas and five percent in Asia. In a change from normal operating methods, Nespresso capsules are not sold in stores and forty-seven percent of sales are currently online, thirty-five percent are from their boutiques, and eighteen percent by the phone.[67]

Nestle clearly understands the global/ local marketplace, and the need to alter its marketing strategies throughout the world. Eastern culture versus western culture, emerging economy versus established economy; all variables cause changes in strategy, entry mode, tastes, pack sizes, and management expertise levels needed.

Key Findings:

- Nestle SA is the largest food manufacturing company in the world, with over 283,000 associates, revenues of US$ 109.9 billion, net profit of US$ 18.04 billion, and organic growth of 3.5 percent.
- Nestle operates in over eighty-six countries, with 8,000 brands, and 29 of those brands returning sales over US$ 1 billion.
- Nestle has a set of ethical and standard operating guidelines that must be used by every employee in every country. The Nestle standard comes first. The brand essence is then protected with these guidelines.
- Nestle has global brands and local brands. Nestle also has global tastes and local tastes. The needs of the local consumer drive the actions regarding tastes, sizes, ingredients, and even how the items are distributed. For example, over 90 percent of the Nestle products in China are produced in China.
- Nestlé's program "Popularly Positioned Products (PPP)" is a standard operating program, which brings the best quality, most highly nutritious foods and beverages within reach of billions of people at the "base of the pyramid".
- Nestle adds iodine to its products in Mexico to battle anemia, sells bouillon cubes in Africa by the each to adjust to the poverty levels, and improves the Milo carbohydrate mix in Malaysia to optimize energy release.
- Nestle uses local market research and local employees to gain market intelligence and operate properly.
- Nestle expatriates are immersed in their new country's culture, are offered private schooling, housing allowances, and generous home leave, in order to bring the best management to offices throughout the world.
- Social and viral marketing are important to Nestle, but the return on investment is still being determined.
- Nestle exists to serve the customer.

Discussion Questions

1. What is your favorite global Nestle product? Your favorite local Nestle product?
2. Nestle states that food is about taste and non-food is about use. Do you agree? Explain your answer.
3. Do you agree with Nestle spending so much focus on sustainability, ethics, morals, and common operating guidelines. Explain your answer.
4. Why does Nestle sell bouillion cubes in jars in the United States and by the cube in Africa? Would you suggest a different direction?
5. What has happened to the Nespresso brand in the last five years? Would you say it is a success? What are your success measures?
6. In a store, take a Nestle product and make suggestions to change either the packaging, shelving location, or how it competes. Explain your answer.
7. Why would Nestle go through the effort to take salt *out* of products sold in the United States and *add* salt into products sold in Africa?
8. What are Nestle's barriers to entry versus their competition?

Case Two- Procter and Gamble

At over US$ 84 billion in revenue and over US$ 12 billion in net income, Procter and Gamble is the eight largest corporation in the world, and ranks among the top companies each year in Fortune's Most Admired Companies list.[68] When William Procter and James Gamble married sisters Olivia and Elizabeth Norris in Cincinnati in 1857, they quickly became business partners.[69] By 1859, sales had reached over US$ 1 million. As business expanded, Procter and Gamble enhanced its assortment by adding Crisco in 1911.

Radio shows in the 20's and 30's called "soap operas" after their main sponsor, additions of Tide detergent in 1946, Prell shampoo in 1950, Crest toothpaste in 1955, Charmin bath tissue in 1957, Downy fabric softener in 1960, Bounce fabric softener sheets in 1972, Pampers diapers in 1961, and then Folgers Coffee, Norwich Eaton Pharmaceuticals, Richardson-Vicks, Noxell, Old Spice, Max Factor and Iams continued their expansion. In 2005, Procter and Gamble announced a major acquisition of Gillette, which catapulted Procter and Gamble to one of the top spots of consumer product goods companies, unseating Unilever. By adding Gillette, Procter and Gamble added Duracell batteries, Braun, and Oral B, as well as the full line-up of Gillette shaving products.[70]

Procter and Gamble has over twenty-four "billion dollar" brands, where each of those brands accounts for over US$ 1 billion in sales on its own. These brands include: Always, Ariel, Actonel, Bounty, Braun, Crest, Dawn, Downy/Lenor, Duracell, Fusion, Gain, Gillette, Head and Shoulders, Old Spice, Ivory, Nice n Easy, Olay, Oral B, Pampers, Pantene, Prilosec, Pringles, Puffs, Secret, TAG, Tide, Vicks, Wella, and Whisper. These products are available on nearly every continent, with manufacturing operations in the United States, Canada, Latin America, Europe, China, Africa, and Australia.[71]

Around the world:

> ➢ Procter and Gamble adopted a new logo after a 1980's controversy surrounding the moon and stars logo being considered satanic. This logo is still used in China and Japan, but only at the end of advertisements.[72]

- In 1980, Procter and Gamble's tampon Rely was implicated in being so absorbent that it was causing increased fluid in the vagina, which was leading to Toxic Shock Syndrome. The company quickly recalled the product from the market.[73]
- In 2007, a class action lawsuit in Georgia alleged users of Crest Pro Health mouthwash suffered stained teeth and lost their sense of taste.[74]
- University of Massachusetts Amherst researchers indentified Procter and Gamble as the 52nd largest corporate producer of air pollution in the United States, with approximately 350,000 pounds of toxic chemicals released annually into the air.[75] In 2007, Procter and Gamble pledged to reduce carbon emissions, mainly through packaging reductions, by 10 percent by 2012.[76]
- Procter and Gamble is one of the founding members of Carbon Disclosure Project's Supply Chain Leadership Council. Procter and Gamble is one of twelve companies on the council. The council's primary aim is to address greenhouse gas emissions and climate change.[77]
- Procter and Gamble funds a recycling school in Cairo, Egypt, which teaches about the business and economics of recycling to the villagers.[78]
- In 2008, the United States Environmental Protection Agency's Design for Environment program awarded Procter and Gamble its highest level of recognition, for the company's work in developing safer detergents under the Safer Detergents Stewardship Initiative.[79]

In China, Procter and Gamble offers a budget detergent called Tide Clean White for the rural areas and offers Tide Triple Action for the urban areas. For each area of China, Procter and Gamble also alters its selling and marketing tactics. In the cities, the company sponsors a reality television show called Absolute Challenge, which has featured contestants vying to win a job as a product representative for Crest or Cover Girl. In the rural areas, Procter and Gamble blankets the smaller mom and pop stores with advertising materials emphasizing the value offered by Tide Clean White and low-end versions of Crest and Oil of Olay skin cream.[80]

We conducted an interview with Tim Penner, President of Procter and Gamble Canada, the topics specifically focused on Procter and Gamble's international operating procedures, localization efforts, and global versus local principles.

The following is a recap of the interview:

Question 1: How does your company handle the various cultural differences across borders?

Response: It is critical for us to understand local culture and local habits and practices in our categories of business. We count on local people to do that for us. As our company has matured, we have drastically reduced the number of expatriates we use as part of our staffing plan. We then drive one common business culture across all countries. I have attached a PowerPoint presentation (described below, after interview) on our Purpose, Values, and Principles (PVP). These guidelines are ingrained into everyone globally, and referred to frequently.

Question 2: Does your company have a specific means of sharing local values with expatriates you send to various countries?

Response: Expatriates who are moving to countries with major cultural differences receive three to five days of training on culture from an outside supplier. They also receive ongoing language training.

Question 3: Does your company value or participate in bringing inpatriates into the existing global management team?

Response: Yes, our senior leadership team is truly global and very diverse.

Question 4: Does your company have different strategies for emerging versus established markets?

Response: Yes, we divide the world into "developed" and "developing" markets. Strategies are different, Research and Development is different, and marketing and supply chain are different.

Question 5: When your company enters a country, is the ability to work with (and possibly assimilate) the existing cultures a consideration (or is the business opportunity the primary consideration)?

Response: All factors are taken into account. When we enter a market, it is for the long term.

Question 6: What steps have been implemented to communicate your existing company values into the new business office, especially if merging with an existing local office?

Response: See the Purpose, Values, and Principles comment (in the section below the questions).

Question 7: How do you ensure that expatriates are rewarded for their willingness to move their families to foreign countries, and what types of people fit the mold for becoming expatriates?

Response: In our company, it is almost impossible to rise to the General Manager level without succeeding in one or more international assignments. One of the "success factors" we measure people against in their performance appraisals is "Builds Diverse Collaborative Relationships". This includes criteria like Inclusiveness, Collaborates, Partners Externally, Builds Networks, and Respects Others. People who rate poorly against these criteria simply do not get ahead.[81]

Procter and Gamble's Purpose, Values, and Principles:

> **Our Purpose:** We will provide branded products and services of superior quality and value that improve the lives of the world's consumers, now and for generations to come. As a result, consumers will reward us with leadership sales, profit, and value creation, allowing our people, our shareholders, and the communities in which we live and work to prosper.

> **Our Values:** Procter and Gamble is its people and the values by which we live. We attract and recruit the finest people in the world. We build our organization from within, promoting and rewarding people without regard to any difference unrelated to performance. We act on the conviction that the men and women of Procter and Gamble will always be our most important asset.

> **Our Values:** Integrity, leadership, ownership, passion for winning, and trust.

> **Leadership:** We are all leaders in our area of responsibility, with a deep commitment to deliver leadership results. We have a clear vision of where we are going. We focus our resources to achieve leadership objectives and strategies. We develop the capability to deliver our strategies and eliminate organizational barriers.

> **Ownership:** We accept personal accountability to meet the business needs, improve our systems and help others improve their effectiveness. We all act like owners, treating the company's assets as our own and behaving with the company's long-term success in mind.

> **Integrity:** We always try to do the right thing. We are honest and straightforward with each other. We operate within the letter and spirit of the law. We uphold the values and principles of Procter and Gamble in every action and decision. We are data-based and intellectually honest in advocating proposals, including recognizing risks.

> **Passion for winning:** We are determined to be the best at doing what matters most. We have a healthy dissatisfaction with the status quo. We have a compelling desire to improve and to win in the marketplace.

- ➢ **Trust:** We respect our Procter and Gamble colleagues, customers and consumers, and treat them as we want to be treated. We have confidence in each other's capabilities and intentions. We believe that people work best when there is a foundation of trust.
- ➢ **Our Principles:** We show respect for all individuals. We believe that all individuals can and want to contribute to their fullest potential. We value differences. We inspire and enable people to achieve high expectations, standards, and challenging goals. We are honest with people about their performance.
- ➢ **The Interests of the Company and the Individual are Inseparable:** We believe that doing what is right for the business with integrity will lead to mutual success for both the company and the individual. Our quest for mutual success ties us together. We encourage stock ownership and ownership behavior.
- ➢ **We are Strategically Focused in our Work:** We operate against clearly articulated and aligned objectives and strategies. We only do work and only ask for work that adds value to the business. We simplify, standardize and streamline our current work whenever possible.
- ➢ **Innovation is the Cornerstone of our Success:** We place great value on big, new consumer innovations. We challenge convention and reinvent the way we do business to better win in the marketplace.
- ➢ **We are Externally Focused:** We develop superior understanding of consumers and their needs. We create and deliver products, packaging, and concepts that build winning brand equities. We develop close, mutually-productive relationships with our customers and our suppliers. We are good corporate citizens. We incorporate sustainability into our products, packaging and operations.
- ➢ **We Value Personal Mastery:** We believe it is the responsibility of all individuals to continually develop themselves and others. We encourage and expect outstanding technical mastery and executional excellence.
- ➢ **We Seek to be the Best:** We strive to be the best in all areas of strategic importance to the company. We benchmark our performance rigorously versus the very best internally and externally. We learn from both our successes and our failures.
- ➢ **Mutual Interdependency is a Way of Life:** We work together with confidence and trust across business units, functions, categories, and geographies. We take pride in results from reapplying others' ideas. We build superior relationships with all parties who contribute to

fulfilling our Corporate Purpose, including our customers, suppliers, universities, and governments.

> **Our Vision:** Be recognized as the best consumer products and services company in the world.
> **Our Promise:** Three billion times a day, Procter and Gamble brands touch the lives of people around the world. And Procter and Gamble people work to make sure those brands live up to their promise to make everyday life just a little bit better, now and for generations to come.[82]

Similar to Nestle, Procter and Gamble has found that establishing global guiding principles has eliminated the ethical, moral, and managerial guess-work inside each office in each country. Different from Nestle, Procter and Gamble primarily trades in non-foods products. Where food products will fall under scrutiny of local tastes, non-food products can be similar throughout the world. The primary considerations center upon usage, size allotments per package, and skin complexion.

Key Findings:

> Procter and Gamble is a US$ 84 billion company, with net income of US$ 12 billion.
> The company possesses twenty-four brands which return over US$ 1 billion each.
> In China, Procter and Gamble offers an opening price point detergent for the lower demographic, another price point type for urban areas, and various other versions of products that will appeal to rural, urban, low income, high income, and middle income.
> The company counts on local people to help it understand local cultures and nuances. The goal is to staff local offices with local associates.
> The company divides the global countries into "developed" and "developing", with differing strategies, research and development, marketing, and supply chains.

Discussion Questions

1. Why is it easier for Procter and Gamble to use the same type products across multiple countries than a company like Nestle or Kraft?
2. Procter and Gamble uses considerable resources to focus on their pollution impact as well as caring for their associates. Is this money well allocated? Why or why not?
3. What are three things you would change about Procter and Gamble's current strategies?
4. What are four differentiators built into the product assortment of Procter and Gamble, which form barriers to entry versus its competitors?
5. From a store visit, what is different about Procter and Gamble's items than those of Kraft or Nestle?
6. How would strategies differ between developed and developing countries?
7. How does Procter and Gamble address different demographic levels in their product assortment?
8. Subsequent to this case, Procter and Gamble sold off Pringles. Would you have sold Pringles? Why or why not?
9. Should Procter and Gamble seek to improve their customers' lives, or just satisfy their demands? Explain.
10. As a retailer, would you rather work with Procter and Gamble or Nestle?

Case Three- AB InBev

AB InBev is a multi-national company formed by the combination of InBev and Anheuser-Busch. As the largest brewing company in the world, AB InBev commands center stage in most of its operating counties. Bob Lachky, vice president of brand management at Anheuser Busch, defines the brand as "a unique or differentiated product or service that has an identifiable image or personality, brought to life through a powerful relationship with a customer."[83]

We conducted an interview conducted with Doug Corbett, President InBev International in the United States, specifically focused on InBev's international operating procedures, localization efforts, and global versus local principles.

The following is a recap of the interview:

Question 1: How does your company handle the various cultural differences across borders?
Response: InBev is truly a global company, with operations in over thirty countries and over 80,000 employees. I am a Canadian citizen, so I am considered an expatriate throughout most of our operating areas.

Question 2: Does your company have a specific means of sharing local values with expatriates you send to various countries?
Response: We will only transfer high achievers globally. Those expatriates will show the local office our company cultures, and they are then charged with learning the local cultures and finding the blend between them.

Question 3: Does your company value or participate in bringing inpatriates into the existing global management team?
Response: At InBev, we only consider people for international assignments who are at Director level and up. We choose the strongest performers only, due to the fact that moving someone internationally is very expensive and risky. These people must have a clear understanding of the InBev system and its culture, the ability to interact with other cultures and be flexible, and we use English as a common language. There is no common template to use, other than the ability to demonstrate leadership in a unique and changing setting.

Question 4: Does your company have different strategies for emerging versus established markets?

Response: We first determine how we will achieve local success in all situations, no matter the type of country. Then, we focus on that success. We have a loyalty to our customers. In the Ukraine, we focus on price. In Korea, we focus on advertising and marketing. Many of our actions are driven by the local competition, and how we can be successful.

Question 5: When your company enters a country, is the ability to work with (and possibly assimilate) the existing cultures a consideration (or is the business opportunity the primary consideration)?

Response: There is quite a difference between Middle Eastern cultures, Asian cultures, and Anglo cultures. At InBev, we utilize a standardized way of going to market and doing business. All of our key performance indicators are the same throughout the world, although interpretations may be different. We look at profit potential first when entering a country, plus how culture is going to impact how we go to market. If Muslims do not drink, we obviously need to tailor our product to a non-alcoholic customer base. We have 30,000 employees in China.

Question 6: What steps have been implemented to communicate your existing company values into the new business office, especially if merging with an existing local office?

Response: At InBev, we will send high performers to offices throughout the world. We ensure that anyone transferring spends many days with relocation specialists to see the area, schools, where to live, etcetera. They are always requested to bring their spouse. They then have access to this relocation agency for the next six months. In this way, the transferred person can espouse the InBev principles into the foreign office while feeling comfortable in their surroundings.

Question 7: How do you ensure that expatriates are rewarded for their willingness to move their families to foreign countries, and what types of people fit the mold for becoming expatriates?

Response: This question was answered above when describing the types of people who are able to transfer throughout the world. After all the training, you then just have to throw the person into the fire and go for it. Certain core competencies are relevant throughout the world.[84]

To gather even more insight into AB InBev's global operating strategies, we conducted an interview with Steve Burrows, CEO and President of Anheuser Busch Asia. In this interview, we wanted to understand Anheuser Busch's views on how an international brand like Budweiser can be tailored to specific markets, like Asia and Africa; where local tastes are addressed while fully utilizing the international branding ability of Anheuser Busch.

Here is a recap of the discussion:

Question 1: How do you determine when a brand should be locally altered or keep consistent traits in all markets?

Response: Unless there are specific legal or regulatory requirements in a country, we do not alter the Bud recipe. It is the same worldwide.

Question 2: In what way has Anheuser Busch adapted brands to emerging economies versus established economies?

Response: In the case of Budweiser, as mentioned, the liquid target is consistency around the world and we invest a good deal in this from shipping raw materials, to placing a brew master on site, and using refrigerated containers when exporting to foreign countries from the United States. We have developed a few brands for local markets. For example, Bud Non Alcoholic for Saudi Arabia, Bud Ultra Low Alcohol for China, and Bud Genuine Draft for China.

Question 3: In countries with low per capita income, what is the main focus of the brands?

Response: I would need to know the specific countries. I do not think we sell beer in countries with very low per capita income, because I suspect that alcohol is not a high priority food item for local residents.

Question 4: Even in low income demographic markets, do you try to address the innate aspirational needs in each consumer? After survival needs, do you still find that teens are as connected as in established economies?

Response: We do not advertise or market to teenagers anywhere in the world. In most countries, the drinking age is 18 or 21, and we aim our marketing and selling at this age category.

Question 5: Have you identified "customer leaders" in your psychographic target markets to become your social spokespeople?

Response: We do not call it that, but we clearly know who the target consumer for our brands are; based upon our own consumer and consumption research and analysis.

Question 6: What is your primary data source in determining brand positioning in each country?

Response: We utilize existing syndicated data where it exists and then our own proprietary research to fill in gaps or sharpen knowledge.[85]

AB InBev has gone through multiple changes in its development. Purchasing Anheuser Busch, the largest brewer in the United States, AB InBev has tackled a monumental task that will take a tremendous amount of its expertise and resources. It will now be operating America's largest brewer, but it will not be American-owned. All of the localization learned throughout the years will be put to the test in the near future. AB InBev thinks of each local market as its own entity, while also understanding that a product like Budweiser cannot change from country to country. The balancing line comes from local intelligence and local tastes, and how those variables can play into the overall global marketing strategy.

Key Findings:

- ➤ AB InBev has operations in over thirty countries and over 80,000 associates. Only high achievers are eligible to transfer globally, as the costs are extremely high. The cost of the move is only a small portion of the costs. The cost of failure is exorbitant.
- ➤ There is a common guiding principle outline that is used by each member of AB InBev. In order to manage an AB InBev office anywhere in the world, you must have a full command of the AB InBev methods of operating and the AB InBev system.
- ➤ For example, the Ukraine focuses on price and Korea focuses on marketing and advertising. Two different local situations driving two different strategies.
- ➤ The recipe for Budweiser remains the same throughout the world. Either the company will employ a brew master in the local office (if large enough), or will ship their product from a nearby operating country.
- ➤ Social and viral media are used where possible. The value is present. The use of social media to sell products is mostly limited by the age requirements for legally purchasing the products.

Discussion Questions

1. InBev bought Anheuser-Busch, the leading United States brewer at the time. What steps would you take to ensure Anheuser-Busch's products could gain from global synergies but still be seen as local by those in the United States?

2. What is happening inside the beer industry in the United States that would challenge traditional brands like Budweiser?

3. What are four strategies you would implement globally at AB InBev to leverage the aggregated scale from being the largest brewer in the world?

4. From a visit to a store, what suggestions would you make to AB InBev's product line to gain even more brand connection?

5. From your own research, what suggestions would you make to AB InBev's marketing to ensure connectivity with each generation?

6. AB InBev does not change taste profiles across the globe, but Kraft Foods does. Who is right? Explain your answer.

7. If you were competing against AB InBev, and you owned a craft brewer in Upstate New York, what are some of the strategies and tactics you would employ to be successful?

8. Is bigger necessarily better? Explain your answer.

9. When using internal data to determine success, what are some of the pitfalls?

10. What ethical and socially-relevant challenges are unique to AB InBev's business that you would not find in other commodities?

Case Four- Unilever

Unilever, founded in 1930, is a British and Dutch company which produces many global brands in food, beverages, cleaning supplies, and personal care products. Unilever employs over 174,000 associates with global revenue of US$ 81 billion[86] and net income of US$ 10.4 billion. Unilever products are represented in over one hundred fifty countries, and are chosen by consumers over 150 million times per day.[87] Unilever started in 1930 by combining the two companies British soap maker Lever Brother with Dutch margarine producer Margarine Unie. Palm oil was a raw material for both soap and margarine. This was one of the first examples of aggregating buying volume to lower costs of goods.

As Unilever grew, it acquired and then disposed of A&W Restaurants in Canada, and acquired Brooke Bond (makers of PG Tips tea). In 1987, Unilever acquired Cheesebrough-Ponds, the makers of Ragu, Pond's, Aqua-Net, Cutex Nail Polish, and Vaseline. In 1989, Unilever acquired Calvin Klein Cosmetics, Faberge, and Elizabeth Arden. By 1996, Unilever acquired Helene Curtis Industries, a major producer of shampoo and deodorant; and added Suave and Finesse hair care products along with Degree deodorant. In 2000, Unilever acquired Best Foods, Ben and Jerry's, and Slim Fast.[88]

Unilever operates companies and factories on every continent except Antarctica, along with research laboratories in England, the Netherlands, Connecticut, New Jersey, India, Pakistan, and in China. For one example of global umbrellas combining with local brands, almost all of Unilever's ice cream business is done under the "Heartbrand" brand umbrella. The name comes from the heart-shaped logo. Unilever operates eleven ice cream factories in Europe, including Germany, Italy, France, and the United Kingdom. The Heartbrand, launched in 1999, was an effort to "increase national brand awareness and promote cross-border synergies in manufacturing and marketing centralization". The Heartbrand logo is present in over forty countries. Although the logo is used worldwide, each country retained its local brand so as to maintain the local familiarity built over the years.

Previous to using the heart logo, each operating country was choosing its own logo. The most common logo was a blue circle with the local brand's name over the background of red and white stripes. Unilever manufactures the same ice cream with the same names, with rare situations of regional availability, under different brands. Some of those situations are Carte D'Or, Cornetto, Magnum, Solero, and Viennetta.[89]

Around the world:

> Unilever was targeted by Greenpeace United Kingdom, for buying palm oil from vendors that were damaging Indonesian rain forests. Unilever is a founding member of the Roundtable on Sustainable Palm Oil, and has a public plan to obtain its palm oil from sustainable sources by 2015.[90]
> Around 50 percent of the tea for Lipton Yellow Label and PG Tips in Western Europe was sourced from Rainforest Alliance Certified farms in 2008.
> All 22,000 products in the food and beverage portfolio are under regular review as part of Unilever's Nutrition Enhancement Programme. Forty-three percent are now in line with internationally accepted guidelines for saturated and trans fat, sugar, and salt.
> Unilever achieved a 1.6 percent reduction in CO_2 from energy per ton of production in manufacturing from 2007-2008, representing a 39 percent reduction since 1995.
> Unilever achieved a 3 percent reduction in water use per ton of production in manufacturing from 2007-2008, representing a 63 percent reduction since 1995.[91]
> In India, Unilever was criticized by Corpwatch for not living up to its environmental standards when operating in India as Hindustan Unilever. According to *The Telegraph*, Hindustan Unilever had to withdraw television advertisements for its women's skin lightening cream, Fair and Lovely. Ads showed lonely, depressed, dark skinned women, ignored by employers and men. Suddenly they found new boyfriends and great careers once the cream lightened their skin.
> Unilever was accused by Greenpeace of allowing Hindustan Unilever to dump multiple tons of very toxic mercury waste in the tourist report of Kodaikanal, and the surrounding Pambar Shola, in Southern India. Greenpeace closed off the contaminated dump site to protect the people from the open mercury waste.[92]
> The Campaign for Commercial Free Childhood lambasted Unilever in 2007 for its Axe marketing campaign considered to be sexist. The sexism was the opposite of the message conveyed through the Dove

campaign that showed women as beautiful even as they are overweight or not perfect models.[93]

> Unilever was named a food industry category leader in the Dow Jones Sustainability World Indexes for the tenth year running- the only company to have ever achieved this distinction.[94]

Previous Unilever Chairman, Michael Treshchow, had a penchant for innovation and localization. As quoted, Treschow liked "inventions, gadgets, and new whizz-bang things.". Treschow stated, "The single most important thing is that we speed up our innovation machine, which means that we bring more highly appreciated products to the consumer so that they say, "Wow, this is really something that I would like to have.".

In regards to global marketing, Treschow is quoted as saying:

> In Italy, there are many risottos. You can bring innovation to any product, from ice cream to mayonnaise to shampoo to deodorant. The point is to bring more consumers to the table.

> How can you convince the Asians to use deodorant? There are a couple of billion people in Asia not using deodorant.

> The point of innovation is to be able to sell the little things to many more millions of people who did not realize that they wanted to have those little things in the first place.

> Asians prefer to make their own soup; they don't buy ready soup. How can you make a platter of components to make it easier to make soup?

> Asia is the great battleground for Unilever in its never-ending war with its multi-national arch rivals, Nestle and Procter and Gamble.

> In 2005, in a response to global competition, Unilever launched One Unilever, and began eliminating duplication, shortening managerial reporting lines and abolishing national head offices.

> Treschow sees the Unilever culture as very European, which involves too much discussion time. He spent time in the United States, to bring a management style that is "very disciplined, very hierarchical, and very focused."

> Treschow is a Swede at the top of an Anglo-Dutch company run by an executive team that includes a Frenchman, two Indians, and an American. Still, Treschow laments, "Unilever has too few women, and we need more Asians, more Asian women."[95]

In January of 2009, Paul Polman was named the new Unilever Chairman. Under Polman's watch, Unilever sold off the United States laundry business to Sun Products Corporation, sold Lawry's to McCormick and Company, and sold Bertolli Oil to Groupo SOS.[96]

Perry Yeatman, of Unilever sees global branding in this manner:

"The one word of advice is to be cautious and understand that there is not one answer. What will work in one culture with one brand may totally flop in another. To be truly successful, the culture and the brand are undoubtedly unique. There is little logic in trying to copy them."[97] In the emerging country of India, Unilever introduced an inexpensive powder detergent called Wheel and outsourced its production to a local manufacturer. Unilever eventually introduced this product in various other emerging countries.[98]

We conducted an interview with Jeffrey Allgrove, Senior Vice President, Unilever Brand Integration. In this interview, we specifically focused on Unilever's international operating procedures, localization efforts, and global versus local principles.

The following is a recap of the interview:

Question 1: How does your company handle the various cultural differences across borders?
Response: We call ourselves a multinational multilocal company. By this, we mean that wherever possible, we take advantage of the fact that we operate in nearly every country in the world, but recognize that we need to adapt to local differences. These differences manifest themselves in several examples:
(1) Markets and products: The taste of tea is different in Russia from Arabia from the United Kingdom. Our blends have to reflect this even though they might be marketed under the same brand name and virtually identical packaging; or the fact that the physical composition of hair is different in Thailand from Italy, so the shampoo formulation has to be different; or the fact that some countries have predominantly hard water and others soft, so the detergent has to be different to work properly.
(2) Advertising: Culturally, some countries are culturally averse to semi-naked women in advertising, whereas in others, it is commonplace (e.g. France, Brazil) so our advertising is adapted to match – normally on the conservative side to allow one advertisement for all.

(3) Workplace cultures: Different laws and cultures are reflected in our various workplaces – and the examples are legion. Clearly we cannot have female drivers in Arabia. You should be able to visit any Unilever site and know that it is Unilever, even though the different manifestations look somewhat different in detail. Our operations are guided by our Code of Business Principles (available on our website), which are applicable everywhere without exception.

Question 2: Does your company have a specific means of sharing local values with expatriates you send to various countries?

Response: There are cultural acclimatization courses run externally to which expatriates can be sent (particularly with their spouses) if the cultural differences are so great that it is warranted. Normally, however, we rely on local induction programmes on arrival.

Question 3: Does your company value or participate in bringing inpatriates into the existing global management team?

Response: Yes, we operate on the basis that an expatriation (inpatriation) is of value both to the business as well as to the individual. Indeed, the terms are somewhat outdated since management cadre is now much more internationalized than in the past, so working with people from other cultures is commonplace.

Question 4: Does your company have different strategies for emerging versus established markets?

Response: Our strategies are determined by category and then country, by first assessing category attractiveness and opportunity. On this basis, we may decide that a category is so attractive and our ability to win so good that a category is designated priority globally. This would accord it first priority on resources everywhere. Mostly, this is not the case, and so the category will be assessed on a country by country basis, and so on. It is important for the allocation of resources. We have about forty category/ country combinations which are of the highest significance. Others might be allocated roles to maintain market share, or generate cash even if some market share is sacrificed. In the nature of things, the developing countries (particularly China, India, Brazil, Mexico, Turkey, Indonesia, and etcetera) have the highest growth opportunities, and therefore feature highly in these priorities, provided that the category is attractive there. But, the strategy per se is not different. In addition, of course, we have to assess risk. We limit resource allocation to say Russia, because although the risk of not building a good business there is high, the risk of putting too much investment there is also high.

Question 5: When your company enters a country, is the ability to work with (and possibly assimilate) the existing culture a consideration (or is the business opportunity the primary consideration)?

Response: The business opportunity is paramount, within our Code of Business Principles. If the environment is too hostile, we will not enter, or will withdraw. For example, if the only way business can be done is to bribe politicians, then we will withdraw as happened in Cameroon in the 1990's.

Question 6: What steps have been implemented to communicate your existing company values into a new business office, especially if merging with an existing local office?

Response: Through our Code of Business Principles, and through the Leader's personal communication.

Question 7: How do you ensure that expatriates are rewarded for their willingness to move their families to foreign countries, and what types of people fit the mold for becoming expatriates?

Response: We have recently changed our international mobility policy such that, in general, expatriates are rewarded in the same way as if they were in their home country. However, some additional reward is given for the fact that they are overseas. In general, the actual reward will allow them to live in the manner to which a typical expatriate at their level will live in the country of inpatriation. This is in contrast to our old system, which gave specific allowances for expatriation. Because of the changing world, this is now considered too generous when benchmarked against market practice. As we "localize" our business further, we expect to have less expatriates, and will build an international cadre to deal with business globally.

Question 8: In the course of acquiring businesses, does Unilever find it is advantageous to leave the newly acquired business alone, or to integrate it quickly?

Response: Finally, the fact is that if we buy a company, we normally have done so because it is unique, and often we say that we want to adopt more of their culture, e.g. Bestfoods. We went to extraordinary lengths to openly post all jobs in the combined business, and have incumbents reapply for their jobs. However, after two years, not many of the management of Bestfoods were left. We have also left acquired businesses alone (e.g. National Starch, Calvin Klein, Slim Fast) which allows the business to continue uninterrupted. When the business is left alone, it makes the acquisition merely a financial investment. Our experience has been that while this can continue successfully for some time, sometimes for a period of many years, it eventually breaks down. If the company gets into trouble, we can no longer afford to leave it alone, and then, of course, it is the worst time to intervene! So, the answer to your question is difficult. We have normally found that it is best to bite the bullet up front, integrate the business, and get on with it. If we can convince the employees and management that we have something to offer, then they will stay and make a contribution to the new business. If not, they will not.[99]

Unilever is a global company with very similar operating methods as Nestle and Procter and Gamble. The company has established enterprise-wide guidelines which will help in determining appropriate ethical and managerial direction. The term "multi-national, multi-local" is a valid term in describing how Unilever thinks of the world considering local tastes, local products, local needs, and aggregated marketing and buying power.

Key Findings:

- Unilever is a US$ 81 billion company with net income of US$ 10.4 billion. Unilever products are represented in over one-hundred fifty countries and are chosen 150 million times per day.
- The company operates offices and factories on every continent except Antarctica, along with research laboratories in England, the Netherlands, Connecticut, New Jersey, India, Pakistan, and China.
- Unilever, similar to Nestle and Procter and Gamble is frequently under scrutiny from activist groups. Greenpeace targeted the company for its palm oil use, Corpwatch criticized Unilever for its lack of environmental standards in India, and the Campaign for Commercial Free Childhood accused the company of being sexist.
- The Chairman values innovation and localization as the keys to future success. Risotto innovation in Italy, deodorant use in Asia, soup preparedness in Asia, are all tops on the list for localization and innovation.
- One quote from the company stated, "There is not one answer (to global branding). What will work in one culture with one brand may totally flop in another. To be truly successful, the culture and brand are undoubtedly unique."
- Unilever thinks of itself as a "multi-national, multi-local" company.
- Markets and products: The taste of tea in Russia is different from Arabia which is different from the United Kingdom. The products keep the same name, but the blends and tastes are different.

- Advertising: Some countries are culturally averse to semi-naked women in advertising; whereas in others, it is commonplace.
- Workplace cultures: Different laws and cultures are reflected in the various workplaces. You should be able to visit any Unilever site and know that it is a division of Unilever.
- Unilever established a Code of Business Principles to be used by all associates throughout the world.
- Unilever tries to hire local managers to run local offices, and sees the role of expatriates fading.
- Strategies are determined by category and then by country, with first category attractiveness and opportunity being assessed. In some countries they are going after market share, in some countries they are trying to maintain market share, and in some countries, they are still establishing the products offered.
- If the business environment is too hostile, they will not enter the country. If you have to bribe politicians to succeed, they will not operate there.
- Entering Russia is an example of the potential payoff ranking higher than the risks. The business opportunity comes first, then the other variables are examined and ranked.

Discussion Questions

1. Unilever is a dominant global company, operating on every continent. What steps have they used to convey their guiding principles across all geographies and all employees?

2. If you were charged with entering a new country for Unilever, and the normal method of operating was through bribing local officials, what would you do? What if it meant you lost your job?

3. In regards to the purchasing of palm oil, what responsibility does Unilever have to solve the ethical issues of producing palm oil?

4. What are four strategies you would implement with Unilever to help them compete in a differentiated way in the United States?

5. What are four strategies you would implement with Unilever to help them compete in a differentiated way in Africa?

6. What is your favorite Unilever product? Why?

7. Why is the word "Unilever" not used in their product names?

8. Would you go to work at Unilever? Why or why not?

9. From visiting a store, what are four suggestions you would make for Unilever's products?

10. What are four suggestions you would make for Unilever's marketing connectivity and effectiveness?

Case Five- Kraft Foods

Before being split into two companies, Kraft Foods was once the largest food and beverage company headquartered in the United States, and second largest in the world after Nestle SA. Philip Morris acquired Kraft in 1988, and merged it with General Foods. Philip Morris then acquired Nabisco and merged it with Kraft. By March, 2007, Kraft had been spun off by Altria (formerly Philip Morris) and now stands as an independent company. Kraft markets its brands in over one-hundred fifty-five countries.[100]

James Kraft started a door to door cheese business in Chicago in 1903. James was then joined by his four brothers to form J.L. Kraft and Brothers in 1909. By 1912, Kraft had a New York headquarters that helped in the global expansion of the brand. By 1914, the company was offering over thirty-one varieties of cheese. In 1915, Kraft had invented pasteurized processed cheese, requiring no refrigeration. In 1919, Kraft made its first acquisition, a Canadian cheese company.

In 1924, the company changed its name to Kraft Cheese Company, and went public. As part of global expansion, Kraft established offices in London and Hamburg in 1927. In 1928, Kraft acquired Phenix Cheese Company, makers of Philadelphia Cream Cheese. Kraft also started operating in Australia after a merger with Fred Walker and Company. In 1930, National Dairy Products Corporation, who made Breyer's Ice Cream and Breakstone's Cottage Cheese and Sour Cream, acquired Kraft-Phenix. During this time, Kraft's products were diversified from solely cheese into salad dressings, caramels, macaroni and cheese dinners, and margarines.

In 1945, Kraft changed its name to Kraft Foods Company, to reflect its diverse product assortment. By the 1960's, Kraft Foods began offering even more assortment, such as jelly, preserves, marshmallows, barbecue sauces, and individually-wrapped cheese slices. In the 1970's Kraft merged with Dart Industries, makers of Duracell batteries, Tupperware plastic containers, West Bend appliances, Wilsonart plastics and Thatcher glass. The new company was called Dart and Kraft. Kraft's food products continued to expand, to include Churney cheeses, Lender's Bagels, Frusen Gladje ice cream and Celestial

Seasonings tea. The non-foods businesses lagged. By the mid-1980's, Kraft had spun off its non-foods business and reverted its focus back to food.

By 1989, Kraft had merged with Philip Morris's General Foods unit, makers of Oscar Mayer meats, Maxwell House coffee, Jell-O gelatin, Budget Gourmet frozen dinners, Entenmann's baked goods, Kool-Aid, Crystal Light, Tang, Post cereals, and Shake 'n Bake flavored coatings. In 1993, Kraft General Foods acquired RJR Nabisco's cold cereal business (Shredded Wheat and Shreddies), while selling its ice cream division to Unilever, and its Birds Eye unit to Dean Foods. In 1994, Kraft General Foods sold its frozen dinners unit to H.J. Heinz.

In 1995, Kraft Foods sold its bakery division (except Lender's Bagels), its candy division, its table spreads division, and Log Cabin syrup. In 2000, Philip Morris acquired Nabisco Holdings for US$ 18.9 billion and merged the company with Kraft. In 2004, Kraft performed some minor sell-offs in sugar confectionary (to Wrigley), hot cereal, pet snacks, juice drinks, functional water, and other grocery brands.[101]

In 2007, Kraft acquired Group Danone's biscuit and cereal divisions for US$ 7.2 billion.[102] Also in 2007, Kraft agreed to sell its cereal unit to Ralcorp Holdings, for US$ 2.8 billion. Kraft's more well-known brands include: A1 Steak Sauce, Arrowroot Biscuits, Bulls Eye Barbeque Sauce, California Pizza Kitchen, Capri Sun, Cheez Whiz, Chips Ahoy, Christie, Cool Whip, Cracker Barrel, DiGiorno, Fig Newtons, Grey Poupon, Jack's Pizza, Jell-O, Kool Aid, Kraft BBQ Sauce, Kraft Macaroni and Cheese, Kraft Mayonnaise, Bagelfuls, Kraft TIGer Biscuits (Malaysia), Lacta (Brazil), Maarud Potato Chips (Norway), Marabou (Sweden), Maxwell House, Milka (Switzerland, Germany, rest of Europe), Miracoli (Germany), O'boy (Scandinavia), Oreo, Oscar Mayer, Taco Bell, Tang, Tassimo, Toblerone, and Velveeta.[103]

We interviewed Dino Bianco, President of Kraft Canada, concerning Kraft's international product standards. The questions asked of Mr. Bianco were as follows:

> ➢ How does your company determine when a product should be locally altered or maintain consistent traits in all markets?
> ➢ In what way has your company adapted products to emerging economies versus established economies?

- In countries with low per capita income rates, what is the main focus of the products?
- Even in low demographic markets, does your company try to address the innate aspirational needs in each consumer? After survival needs, does your company still find that teens are as connected as in established economies?
- How does your company use viral and social networking to connect with consumers?
- Have you identified "ideal customers" in your psychographic target markets to become your social spokespeople?
- What is your primary data source in determining product positioning in each country?

Mr. Bianco replied to the specific product and customer connectivity questions in the following manner:

- Kraft has no hard and fast rules. Food is emotive, so it will have high variability across the global marketplace. We must be flexible to ensure we meet local customer tastes and nuances.
- While health and beauty products or general merchandise is generic and usage-oriented, food is taste-driven and must appeal to local tastes. For example, the Oreo maintains global appeal and marketing, but the inner ingredients vary by country. Philadelphia Cream Cheese is handled in a similar manner. In Maxwell House Coffee, the brand truths remain the same, but the tastes and flavors change by marketplace.
- Forty percent of the Kraft business is done outside North America.
- Oreo, Philadelphia Cream Cheese, Tang, Maxwell House Coffee, Toblerone, and Tassimo are all global brands that started in North America and worked their way across the world.
- For each of the products, the brand foundation, promise, and architecture all remain the same. Two extreme instances are Toblerone, which is the same formula world-wide and Oreo, which is market-specific in tastes.
- In low income areas, powdered drinks like Tang are used for vitamins and sustenance.
- In low income demographic areas, where low per capita earnings are the main issue, Kraft adjusts portion sizes but not quality. In fact, we sometimes add healthy ingredients to help support nutrition-seeking by those with very little money.

- In Kraft Salad Dressing, we operate in North America, the United Kingdom, Germany, and Australia- and all branding and customer connectivity is de-centralized.
- Kraft Dinner is totally different in Canada than in the United States (where it is called Kraft Macaroni and Cheese). The same is true with Miracle Whip.
- Kraft will use just as many differences in advertising and communication across countries.
- The customers' preferences are the primary concern- that's the rule.
- Where we are not the market leader in the country, Kraft looks at the taste profiles as the main reason for lack of success.
- Kraft aligns with creative advertising agencies that are similar in the fact that they are globally-focused and have offices in multiple countries to satisfy local needs.
- In regards to social and viral marketing, Kraft is making in-roads and has recently doubled its budget in this area. Kraft is still lagging. Kraft products are fully integrated, including digital links, but we need improvement.
- The product and brand must be "true" in regards to social and viral marketing, where Kraft will talk about the brand actively. Kraft virally markets Shreddies and Nabob as social brands.
- Social and viral marketing cannot be measured very well, but is a strategic necessity.[104]

We were able to interview Cathy Webster, the Kraft Vice President of Human Resources. The questions I asked were the following:

- How does your company handle the various cultural differences across borders?
- Does your company have a specific means of sharing local values with expatriates you send to various countries?
- Does your company value or participate in bringing inpatriates into the existing global management team?
- Does your company have different strategies for emerging versus established markets?
- When your company enters a country, is the ability to work with (and possibly assimilate) the existing culture a consideration (or is the business opportunity the primary consideration)?

➢ What steps have been implemented to communicate your existing company values into the new business office, especially if merging with an existing local office?

➢ How do you ensure that expatriates are rewarded for their willingness to move their families to foreign countries, and what types of people fit the mold for becoming expatriates?

Cathy Webster responded with the following information:

➢ At Kraft, we focus on the consumer and work from there.
➢ We have a solid International Assignment Policy, which is how we support our people, plus it outlines what we look for in people who would be able to move around globally.
➢ The traits we find the most valuable are: learning agility, flexibility, and learning ability.
➢ The Canadian head of operations is from the United Kingdom.
➢ There are Canadians represented throughout the world, including Australia, Singapore, South Pacific, and Switzerland.
➢ Kraft has moved to a total focus inside each country, with autonomy. We now have a full business inside each business unit.
➢ Dino Bianco runs all of Canada, including finance, marketing, and operations.
➢ Kraft looks for a mix of expats and locals on each team.
➢ All of the Kraft business in the European Union is centralizing in Zurich.
➢ Kraft does not have as much focus on trying to identify Asian abilities versus Anglo abilities. We think that certain success traits can transcend cultural differences.
➢ We have a centralized expat group in Chicago.
➢ The expat group offers to spend time with people who have gone international with Kraft.[105]

Kraft has found the ability to stay true to its brand essence throughout the world, while still adapting to local tastes. Similar to Nestle, Kraft is in the food business, and it would be ill-advised to keep taste-profiles similar across geographies. As seen in the examples of Nestle, Procter and Gamble, and Unilever, Kraft found it necessary to either focus on food or non-foods; but, not focus on both. To market food, you need a localized method of operating upon which a brand profile for the world can be built. To market non-food, you are better served with a focus on usage and demographic nuances, which can then be a part of the global brand profile. The ingredients will not change drastically from country to country.

Key Findings:

> Kraft Foods manufactures many of the world's most well-known food items, including Macaroni and Cheese, Tang, Maxwell House, and Jell-O.

> Before splitting into two separate companies, Kraft Foods was the largest food and beverage company headquartered in the United States. Both Unilever and Nestle have headquarters in Europe.

> There are no "hard and fast rules" to use for marketing its food across the globe. Food is emotive, and is recognized as having high variability in tastes throughout the world's marketplace.

> For example, Oreo maintains global appeal and marketing, but the inner ingredients vary by country. For Maxwell House, the brand truths remain the same, but the tastes and flavors change by marketplace.

> Toblerone is the same formula world-wide, and Oreos change by country. This is similar to Nespresso's (Nestle) being the same world-wide while Nescafe varies by country.

> Customers' preferences are the primary concern- that's the rule.

> Kraft is making in-roads into viral marketing and social media, but feels they are behind where they should be at this point. Kraft virally markets Shreddies and Nabob, while other brands are marketed in "traditional" manners.

> Kraft has an International Assignment Policy, which supports its associates as they transfer from country to country.

> Kraft sees the world as full of foreign interaction, similar to Unilever, where the term "expatriate" is almost archaic. The Canadian head of operations is from the United Kingdom, the European headquarters is located in Zurich, Switzerland, and Eastern versus Western culture is not seen as a major variable anymore.

Discussion Questions

1. Kraft Foods is a dominant global brand, even after splitting into two companies, operating on every continent. What steps have they used to convey their guiding principles across all geographies and all employees?

2. How are the products that are carried by Kraft different than those carried by Procter and Gamble? How do these differences impact their operating procedures, and methods of going to market, by country?

3. What are the pro's and cons to having such a strong expatriate program at Kraft?

4. What are four strategies you would implement with Kraft to help them compete in a differentiated way in the United States?

5. What are four strategies you would implement with Kraft to help them compete in a differentiated way in Japan?

6. What is your favorite Kraft product? Why?

7. Why is the word "Kraft" used in the majority of their product names?

8. Would you go to work at Kraft? Why or why not?

9. From visiting a store, what are four suggestions you would make for Kraft's products?

10. What are four suggestions you would make for Kraft's marketing connectivity and effectiveness?

Case Six - PepsiCo/ Frito Lay

PepsiCo is a multi-national corporation, focused upon Frito-Lay snacks, Pepsi soft drinks and water, in addition to Quaker products like Granola Bars and Gatorade. With 2008 sales exceeding US$ 43 billion and net income exceeding US$ 5 billion, PepsiCo employs over 185,000 associates worldwide. Begun in 1898 by pharmacist and industrialist Caleb Bradham, PepsiCo has been an entrepreneurial and diverse company since its inception. Its history includes Pepsi merging with Frito-Lay in 1965 and becoming known as PepsiCo. Next it formed Yum brands with KFC, Pizza Hut, and Taco Bell. The company sold off Yum Brands in 1997. PepsiCo purchased Tropicana in 1998, and Quaker Oats in 2001. In 2005, Pepsi passed Coca-Cola in market value after competing with each other for one-hundred twelve years. PepsiCo owns five different billion dollar brands: Pepsi, Tropicana, Frito-Lay, Quaker, and Gatorade.[106]

We had the opportunity to interview Marc Guay, President of PepsiCo Canada. In this interview, we were focusing upon the international development and global branding efforts put forth by PepsiCo. Plus, we focused our discussion on the principles and operating guidelines set forth by the PepsiCo headquarters to shape behavior throughout the world.

Excerpts from the interview:

> The PepsiCo culture is one of diversity and inclusion. These nuances are embedded in the operations of every business unit, which makes it easy to embrace global diversity.
> The strict "my way or else" culture, similar to Coke, does not work when entering new markets. This bore truth when Coke had the tainted water scandal in the Middle East, has faced multiple lawsuits and union activity, etc.
> PepsiCo builds its teams from local teams.
> PepsiCo aims to identify people inside the organization based upon the N. D. Pearson book *Muscle Building the Organization*, a story from Harvard Business Review twenty years ago.
> With over one hundred business units, PepsiCo performs a formal review of the bench strength (leadership back-up strength), focuses upon development, targets people who are ready to advance, and

works to understand whether or not they could relocate internationally and operate in multiple countries.

➢ PepsiCo looks at employees on zero to twelve month horizons, as well as twelve to thirty-six month horizons.

➢ Language capability factors into the process of analyzing employees for global transfers.

➢ Employees are grouped into the following:
  o Blockers- People who are not going anywhere and need to grow in their position.
  o Promotable- People who can be promoted one time in the next five years.
  o Future leaders- Employees who can be promoted two times in the next five years.

➢ PepsiCo's goal is to have two people ready to step into every leadership role.

➢ President Marc Guay identified Richard Glover as his replacement and developed a program to allow him plenty of international leadership experience, including sending him to Australia.

➢ In order to address unique local nuances, PepsiCo uses a company named International Management Consultants to help with sensitivity training for the employees and cultural awareness training for the families.

➢ PepsiCo's world is divided in this manner: North America Foods (Frito Lay and Quaker), North America Beverage (Pepsi), and PepsiCo International (seven regions globally).

➢ In England, Walker's chips uses the Frito Lay sun as part of their logo but uses the locally relevant name Walker's.

➢ PepsiCo believes in empowerment and decentralization.

➢ No matter your location, sustained results are the key to success.

➢ PepsiCo has a keen focus on the BRIC countries- Brazil, Russia, India, and China.

➢ Frito Lay brands globally: Lay's in North America, Walker's in the United Kingdom, and Smith's in Australia. Frito Lay has one-hundred fifty global local flavors.[107]

Marc Guay also provided PepsiCo's Values. They are a commitment to deliver sustained growth through empowered people acting with responsibility and building trust. The PepsiCo "guiding principles" are that "We must always strive to care for customers, consumers, and the world we live in; sell only products we can be proud of; speak with truth and candor; balance short term and long term; win with diversity and inclusion; respect others and succeed together.".

Also provided was an outlined session used as a "live" example of a cultural awareness class. This session included the following segments:

- Introduction to Program
- Challenges of Working in Asia
- Improving Communication in Asia
- How Culture Impacts Reality
- The Variety of Culture on a Global Team
- Organization of Chinese and Asian Society
- Modern Asian Facts and Realities
- How Asians Think and Learn- China
- Historical Trends in China
- Modernization and Westernization in Asia
- The Changing Face of Business in China
- Understanding Islam
- Working with Indonesians and Malaysians
- Understanding the Thai
- The Challenge of the Philippines
- Building Strong Interpersonal Relations in Hong Kong
- Protocol in Hong Kong
- Alignment of PepsiCo International in Asia
- Cross-Cultural Stress
- Family Support
- Review and Discussion[108]

PepsiCo throughout the world:

- PepsiCo created a joint venture in India with Punjab Agro Industrial Corporation and Voltas India Limited.[109] It was claimed that this joint venture was formed because PepsiCo was initially denied access to India because it would not provide a list of ingredients of its products. These ingredients are seen as proprietary and competitively protected. As PepsiCo began to operate in India, testing by the Centre for Science and Environment (CSE) claimed that Pepsi contained toxins, such as lindane, DDT, Malathion, and chlorpyrifos.[110]

- Until 1997, PepsiCo was a very successful operator in Burma. Unfortunately, PepsiCo's business partner, Thein Tun, was also a high-ranking partner with the ruling Burmese military junta responsible for egregious human rights violations. PepsiCo was compelled to end its relationship in Burma and pull out of the country.[111]
- PepsiCo was not sold in Israel until 1991, allowing for criticism that it was supporting the Arab boycott of Israel. PepsiCo denied this allegation, stating that the market was too small to support a local franchise. PepsiCo's market share is extremely low in Israel even today.[112]
- PepsiCo announced in August, 2009, that it was acquiring Amacoco, Brazil's largest coconut water company. Coconut water is seen as a natural hydration source, and is extremely popular in Brazil and dozens of countries. Amacoco manufacturers the top selling coconut water brands, Kero Coco and Trop Coco. According Luis Montoya, president of Latin America Beverages, a division of PepsiCo, "This transaction reflects PepsiCo's long-term commitment to investing in Brazil, and we will harness PepsiCo's expertise in marketing, production, and distribution to accelerate the momentum behind Kero Coco and Trop Coco.".[113]

PepsiCo has a clear culture of diversity and inclusion, and seems diligent in its desire to maintain localized tastes and consumer connectivity. PepsiCo is one of the leaders in social and viral marketing. The PepsiCo brands, especially Frito Lay, Pepsi, Mountain Dew, and Dorito's are highly attractive to those aged twelve to twenty; so, they lend themselves to an "alternate media" marketing program. As with the previous consumer goods manufacturers, PepsiCo is a frequent target of consumer groups, and is constantly protecting its brand image throughout the world.

Key Findings:

- PepsiCo is a US$ 43 billion company, with net income exceeding US$ 5 billion. PepsiCo employs over 185,000 associates worldwide.
- The PepsiCo culture is one of inclusion and diversity. PepsiCo's chief rival, Coca-Cola, had a "my way or else" mentality that tended to bring the ire of consumer groups and customers worldwide. PepsiCo learned from their rival, and has a different method of going to market globally.

- PepsiCo aims to form local teams, in order to understand local tastes and nuances. Similar to the previous consumer goods companies, the term "expatriate" is viewed as old-fashioned as the current operating method is to develop employees by transferring them across geographies and product units.

- PepsiCo mentions language capability as a factor in determining which associates can transfer globally. This is the first mention of language abilities from any of the consumer goods companies.

- PepsiCo uses International Management Consultants to help with sensitivity training for the associates and their families.

- PepsiCo divides the world into North America Foods (Frito Lay and Quaker), North America Beverage (Pepsi), and PepsiCo International (seven regions globally).

- PepsiCo is one of the social and viral marketing leaders globally, which will be covered in the chapter on social media.

- Frito Lay chips can be seen as Walker's in the United Kingdom, Lay's in the United States, and Smith's in Australia. They each share the sun as part of their logo, but have maintained their locally-relevant brand names and taste profiles.

- PepsiCo established a set of "guiding principles", to be used by all associates worldwide. These principles are similar to Nestle, Procter and Gamble, and Unilever.

Discussion Questions

1. Pepsico is a major brand on all continents. What steps have they used to convey their guiding principles across all geographies and all employees?
2. Why would Pepsico have used a strategy to incorporate Pepsi, Frito-Lay, and Quaker products under one "brand umbrella"?
3. Why would Pepsico have maintained the original brand names on their products, even after placing all brands under one corporate brand?
4. What are four strategies you would implement with Pepsico to help them compete in a differentiated way in the United States?
5. What are four strategies you would implement with Pepsico to help them compete in a differentiated way in Brazil?
6. What is your favorite Pepsico product? Why?
7. What portion of the obesity crisis, as well as diabetes proliferation, is owned by Pepsico and its products?
8. Would you go to work at Pepsico? Why or why not?
9. From visiting a store, what are four suggestions you would make for Pepsico's products?
10. What are four suggestions you would make for Pepsico's marketing connectivity and effectiveness?

Case Seven- Price Chopper

A retailer or consumer goods company must know itself first, before presenting itself or its services and goods to the global retailing environment. Knowing its true identity will ensure that, in the course of the global marketing operations, a company will not lose its core identity as it grapples with the variables that will present themselves. Below is one example of how a company set forth to establish its identity.

Price Chopper, a retailer of US$ 3.7 billion in retail sales in the northeast United States, set out to change its identity in relation to its customer base and future desired market and branding position. The project was named "Building the Price Chopper Brand of the Future on the Best of our Past." In the following, we will describe the steps taken by Price Chopper in identifying the strength of its current brand, the proposed brand, and a roadmap for solidifying the brand presence in the eyes of its customers.

The first move was to establish the "Eight Steps to Success":

1. Establish current Price Chopper image
2. Define vision of the future
3. Establish mission
4. Define customer segments and core customer focus
5. Establish brand personality and character
6. Brand essence
7. Brand identity
8. Put in place pillars of success[114]

Step One- Establish current Price Chopper image

- ➢ Fundamental strengths to build upon
- ➢ Reflection of information, data, insights and collected to date in research
- ➢ Price Chopper points of parity and points of difference
- ➢ Focus and leverage unique points of difference

As the initial activity in this section, a Strengths, Weaknesses, Opportunities, and Threats (SWOT) analysis was performed:

> **Strengths:** Strong value image of price and quality, quality and selection of fresh foods, promotional and store excitement, strong merchandising and purchasing power, values of the company and people, Golub (family-owned) way of life, and the ability to act like a large chain while staying trim and nimble.

> **Weaknesses:** Lack of defined strategy for the future, no overall brand look or feel, trying to be all things to all people, training and staff issues, store layout and flow, in-store confusion, cleanliness, and lack of overall shopping and buying emotional experience.

> **Opportunities:** Support customers' needs to save time and money and make it easier for them to shop, help make the shopping and buying experience more enjoyable and more emotional, differentiate from the competition by providing added services in fresh, be the "go to" place for the target customers' food needs, and continue to strengthen the value image.

> **Threats:** Threats of unknown in the economy and competition, lower customer spending power, rising costs, lower customer optimism and confidence, strong and growing emphasis on price, major competition moving towards "everyday low price", competition focusing on "easy shop", and a growing list of international competition.

Also in Step One, the major competitor strengths and weaknesses were determined:

> Hannaford:
>   o Strengths: Utilitarian approach succeeds with customers who want a simplified shopping experience, everyday low pricing, store layouts, demonstrated leadership in natural and organics.
>   o Weaknesses: Boring stores, weekly ads, no shopper card.
> Stop and Shop:
>   o Strengths: Strong health and beauty care program, clean stores, and friendly store layout.
>   o Weaknesses: Continual shifts in pricing strategies.
> Wegmans:
>   o Strengths: Reputation, execution excellence, solutions-oriented approach to customers' needs, staff, everyday low pricing, fresh quality and execution, significant store brand program.

- Weaknesses: Size of stores may not be for everyone, limited variety in the center of the store, and price perception.
  - ➤ Wal-Mart:
    - Strengths: one-stop shopping, low price perception, awareness and repositioning of their brand, financial clout.
    - Weaknesses: Size of stores, in-store experience, staff knowledge, fresh departments.

Step Two- Define Vision of Future, where the Brand aspires to be

- ➤ Now: Middle of the pack
- ➤ Future (three years): Leader in shopping experience
- ➤ Future (five years): Store of choice in each market, with core customer versus core competitor

In this section, it was decided that market leadership is assumed to be "holy ground." Top of mind leadership is the goal, and one dominant idea will connect with each customer.

Step Three- Establish Mission

- ➤ Now: Best in Fresh and Value
- ➤ Future (three years): Excitement in the shopping experience. Price Chopper wants to be the first choice for basics plus to be easy to shop, attractive and exciting, and offer helpful and informed service.
- ➤ Future (five years): The customer resource. Price Chopper wants to be the store of choice known for providing helpful people and tools to improve the lives of consumers by continuously satisfying the family's food needs. Price Chopper wants to establish strong customer relationships with established consumer resources.

Step Four- Define Customer Segments and Core Customer Focus

Victoria: Confident traditionalist on a budget, 12 percent of households, average household spend is US$ 205 on groceries every two weeks, thinks meal planning and preparation is important, does not spend a lot of money on groceries.

Victoria's preferred store attributes:

- Quality service in the fresh food department
- Freshness and quality of fruits and vegetables
- Aisles that are kept clear
- The availability of the butcher in the meat department
- Having the weekly flyer and newspaper ads
- Price of advertised specials
- Selection of products for holidays and special occasions

Martha: Affluent experimenter, 16 percent of households, average household spend is US$ 252 on groceries every two weeks, loves to plan meals and cook for her family both everyday and on special occasions, does not stick to a budget, loves to experiment with cooking and considers herself a gourmet cook, does not clip coupons.

Martha's preferred store attributes:

- Quality service in the fresh food department
- Someone is available to answer questions or help her find something
- Quantity of sale items in stock
- Having the weekly ad flyer
- Wide aisles
- Having specialty cheeses

Caitlin: Enthusiastic traditionalist, 14 percent of households, average household spend is US$ 234 on groceries every two weeks, enjoys cooking, particularly enjoys cooking for special events and on weekends, meals tend to be pretty traditional, does not plan menus, does not budget for grocery shopping, wings it, does not read ad flyers, does not clip coupons.

Caitlin's preferred store attributes:

- Having a frequent shopper card that has many benefits
- Having a butcher available in the meat department
- Having a selection of private label or store brands
- Having products for holidays and special occasions

Shared attributes for Victoria, Martha, and Caitlin:

➤ Essential resource to help satisfy my family's food needs
➤ Quality of service in the fresh food departments
➤ Quantity of sale items in stock
➤ Aisles are kept clear
➤ Availability of a butcher in the meat department
➤ Having a weekly ad flyer and shopper loyalty card
➤ Selection of products for holidays and special occasions
➤ Price on advertised specials
➤ Prices are clearly identified
➤ Having wide aisles
➤ Selection of specialty cheeses

Step Five- Brand Personality and Character

Price Chopper current self-perception: Down to Earth, grounded, competitive, reliable, and trustworthy
Price Chopper future self-perception: Friendly, engaging, inspiring, exciting, and trustworthy

➤ Outward face of the Price Chopper brand expressed in human terms
➤ Personality helps the brand come to life and makes it accessible and touchable
➤ Helps to differentiate Price Chopper from the competitors

Character

➤ Inward, internal values of the Price Chopper brand and its culture
➤ Company's commitment made to management, staff, customers, supporters, expressed in each person's own words
➤ Customer-focused, family-oriented, ethical, hard working, passionate, team-oriented, community-minded, trusting, respectful, and proud

Step Six- Brand Essence

Market leadership is the "holy ground":

➤ For the most part, people remember one thing

> Top of mind leadership is Price Chopper's goal
> One dominant idea to become great

Brand essence:
> One idea/ word that we want to own in our customer's mind
> Simple, easily understood and valued
> Not a little about a lot, but a lot about a little
> Helpful- improving lives through our goods, services, and relationships
> Approachable, responsive, knowledgeable, engaging, exciting, convenient, friendly, team oriented, efficient, save time and money

Step Seven- Brand Identity

> What is the internal DNA of the brand?
> It is what we get up everyday to accomplish beyond our functions.
> It is who we are: real, authentic, ingrained in our being.
> Does it come out of the bedrock of the founder's set of shared beliefs?
> It is a reflection of actions more than words.
> Does it have a higher focus or noble cause?
> Are we the customer's hero by providing a more enjoyable food experience, by succeeding in meeting various roles, by reducing stress, by providing value and quality prices, by making the shopping experience more fun, by saving the consumer time, by inspiring ideas, by taking care of the family and food needs, and by helping provide special moments?

Step Eight- Pillars of Success

High-level strategic initiatives to guide and direct each function's tactical and business plans.

Operations
> Develop service culture; both bottom up and top down
> Define store experience (service) from customer's point of view; guardrails for managers and associates
> Empower management to execute programs and hold them accountable with guardrails
> Develop and promote the right skills and attitudes for success among management and staff. Replace the people who do not fit the culture.

- ➢ Create a total service model for the entire store
- ➢ Manage total experience versus functional silos in order to create a holistic experience

Merchandising
- ➢ Establish focus on core customer segments among merchants
- ➢ Use solutions-based merchandising to meet customers' needs and wants
- ➢ Creating news: items, displays, deals, WOW deals
- ➢ Build in-store celebrations around products
- ➢ Simplify- what should be rationalized?
- ➢ Provide cross functional teams to deal with issues and opportunities
- ➢ Focus on corporate brands

Marketing
- ➢ Develop clear brand identity for all stakeholders (customers, associates, trade partners)
- ➢ Communicate internally with holistic approach to entire Price Chopper organization
- ➢ Support internal branding with how's and why's
- ➢ Communicate externally to defined core customers only after it is understood and accepted internally
- ➢ Combination of traditional and new media integration into everything, every touch point
- ➢ Act as the gatekeepers across all functional areas of the company

Next Steps (Developed after the eight-step branding and identity project was completed)

These steps were identified as:

- ➢ Support and buy-in of the brand team and senior team
- ➢ Set corporate pillars of success to align the organization
- ➢ Bring the brand to life with words (brand promise) and visuals
- ➢ Develop internal branding plan to build on best practices- if you cannot measure it, you cannot manage it
- ➢ Develop and detail internal and external communication plan
- ➢ Develop a launch plan, with team, timing, and budgets
- ➢ Use a brand team to kick start the brand process

- Use as context a set of guardrails for development and detailing of the corporate business plan: financial, human resources, people, real estate.
- Annual tracking of brand equity: financial, customer, performance; a total scorecard[115]

The above example of Price Chopper is one salient method of establishing a brand's core identity that can be communicated properly, quickly, and effectively to all associates. The process states succinctly that the associates must know the identity before the public can learn the identity.

Discussion Questions

1. Name four key takeaways from the Price Chopper case.
2. What would you do differently from the above case example?
3. Do you think the plan will work? Explain your answer.
4. In the broader scheme of food retail, where does Price Chopper fit?
5. Who are Price Chopper's main competitors? Identify differentiators that could make Price Chopper standout against each competitor.
6. In your opinion, what are the long-term prospects for Price Chopper in the food industry?
7. Would you shop at Price Chopper?
8. Name two strategies and four tactics you would suggest to Price Chopper.

Case Eight – Tesco

Tesco, operating with its home base in England, was founded in 1919 by Jack Cohen in East London. Being the largest British retailer, with profits exceeding three billion British pounds, Tesco is the third largest retailer in the world, behind Wal-Mart and Carrefour. Tesco carries such goods as food, drinks, clothing, consumer electronics, financial services, telecoms, insurance (home, health, auto), dental plans, retailing and renting DVD's, CD's, music downloads, internet services, and software.[116]

Total sales revenue for the fiscal year ending 2009 was 59.4 billion British pounds, and operating income was 3.128 billion British pounds.[117] The name, Tesco, appeared in 1924, when Jack Cohen bought a shipment of tea from T. E. Stockwell. He made labels with the first three letters of the supplier's name and the first two letters of his surname. The first Tesco store was opened in 1929, and Tesco joined the London Stock Exchange in 1947.[118] Throughout the 1950's and 1960's, Tesco grew to more than eight hundred stores. By 1973, Jack Cohen had resigned, and he had been replaced by his son-in-law, Leslie Porter.[119]

In 1994, Tesco made its foray into Scotland, and the company subsequently introduced its loyalty card and internet shopping. By 1997, Terry Leahy had taken the realm.[120] Also in 1997, Tesco moved into Ireland with an acquisition of Associated British Foods. In 2001, Tesco purchased a 35 percent share of Grocery Works in the United States and purchased thirteen HIT hypermarkets in Poland.[121] In 2003, Tesco purchased the C Two-Network in Japan[122] and acquired a majority stake in Kipa in Turkey.[123] In 2004, Tesco Lotus, a joint venture, was launched in Thailand and Tesco purchased an 80 percent stake in Casino's Leader Price stores in Poland.[124]

In order to ensure it can fit into any marketplace and any situation, Tesco has divided its store formats into six types of stores:

> ➤ **Tesco Extra:** These are large hypermarkets which stock all products.
> ➤ **Tesco Superstore:** This format consists of large supermarkets stocking groceries and a smaller selection of general merchandise.

- ➤ **Tesco Metro:** This banner contains mid-sized stores, between Superstores and Tesco Express stores. These stores are mainly located in city centers, the inner city, and on the high streets of small towns.
- ➤ **Tesco Express:** These stores are mostly neighborhood convenience stores, stocking mainly food with an emphasis on higher-margin products and everyday essentials.
- ➤ **One Stop:** These stores are the only stores without Tesco in their name. These are the smallest stores in the chain.
- ➤ **Tesco Homeplus:** This format is Tesco's foray into a non-food only store.[125]

Tesco's international operations are as follows:

- ➤ **China:** 79 stores. It operates with a 50 percent stake in the Hymall chain from Ting Hsin of Taiwan. Tesco operates mostly near Shanghai and is also operating its Tesco Express format.[126]
- ➤ **Czech Republic:** 113 stores. Tesco entered the Czech Republic by buying the K-Mart stores and converting them to Tesco stores. Tesco operates petrol stations, has an expansive selection of non-foods, and offers personal financial services.
- ➤ **France:** 1 store. It operates one wine, beer and spirits store in Calais, France.[127]
- ➤ **Hungary:** 149 stores. Tesco bought K-Mart's operations in Hungary, and proceeded to open hypermarkets. Tesco offers its full array of store brand items, along with clothing and personal finances.[128]
- ➤ **Republic of Ireland:** 116 stores. Tesco operates regular stores similar to the stores in United Kingdom, offering home delivery, petrol, mobile telephones, personal finance, floral delivery, and a weight loss program. Tesco is the grocery market leader in Ireland.
- ➤ **Japan:** 144 stores. It operates small corner stores after entering Japan on a buyout of C Two stores and Fre'c. Tesco also offers software in Japan.
- ➤ **Malaysia:** 36 stores. It operates Tesco stores and Tesco Extra stores. Tesco entered Malaysia by partnering with a local conglomerate Sime Darby Berhad. The local company still owns 30 percent of the shares. Tesco offers a wholesale line, a value range, electronic goods, the loyalty card, and apparel.

- ➤ **Poland**: 319 stores. Tesco Poland offers the full assortment of store brands produce, petrol, personal financial services, and on-line photo processing.[129]
- ➤ **Slovakia**: 70 stores. Tesco Slovakia opened in 1996, and operates Tesco Express local stores. Tesco Slovakia has a major focus on organic goods.[130]
- ➤ **South Korea**: 347 stores. It operates hypermarkets and the express format, in a partnership with Samsung. Tesco owns 81 percent of the joint venture. Tesco is the largest food retailer in South Korea, but lags behind locals Shotte and Shinsegae Group.[131] In 2008, Tesco purchased thirty-six hypermarkets from Carrefour, making Tesco the second largest retailer in the country.[132]
- ➤ **Thailand**: 607 stores. It operates through a joint venture with Charoen Pokphand, and the operation is called Tesco Lotus. Tesco Lotus offers food, electronics, and personal financial services. Tesco Lotus focuses on local procurement, with 97 percent of its goods sourced from within Thailand.
- ➤ **Turkey**: 99 stores. It operates under the name Kipa, and runs Tesco Express-type stores.
- ➤ **United States**: Previously 115 stores. Tesco operated a chain of convenience stores on the West Coast called Fresh and Easy. Wal-Mart quickly opened its counter-attack to Fresh and Easy, and the road to expansion ended in Tesco selling its stores to Wild Oats.[133]
- ➤ **Total: 2,195 stores**

As an example of the complexity of operating multiple banners across many borders, during one week, Tesco was criticized by an international trade union group over its labor policies in foreign countries, was expanding its price reduction program in Ireland that had been originally introduced at border stores in Dublin, was launching a new ready meal assortment called "City Kitchen" (a trial grouping of food which includes six lines and is at the premium end of the market), was over-hauling its website in England, was launching its second private label beer in Fresh and Easy, was protecting its software in its Tesco India division, was investing over US$ 204 million to rapidly expand in Thailand, was accused in its Thai subsidiary (Tesco Lotus) of abusing workers' rights, and was linked to an early sale of government-owned British Bank Northern Rock (Tesco is interested in owning the bank).

In the week of August 24, 2009, Tesco was preparing to offer mortgages in 2010 as a strategy to take advantage of the opportunity that arose from banks badly affected by the credit crunch, Tesco saw this as an opportunity to offer a "string competitor in the market place". Also in the same week, Tesco was fitting cattle with microphones dubbed "rumination collars", to monitor their belching in a bid to reduce methane emissions, was investing heavily in telepresence equipment from Cisco to bridge the distance between the United Kingdom headquarters and its Indian offshore centre Hindustan Service Centre, and was bringing on a team of six weather professionals to help plan more accurately which types of foods it will need to stock. This team will use the Tesco-developed computer program which will produce detailed weather reports for the entire United Kingdom going back five years and what effects this weather had on individual Tesco store sales.[134]

Tesco has a strategy of always using its own name when acquiring companies in various countries, plus strongly promoting its store brands to gain loyalty and gross profit. Tesco seemingly appeals to all segments of the market. Tesco has set its own purposes, values, principles, and goals throughout the world. This standard, used globally in Tesco, points to Tesco's focus on people, including both customers and employees.[135] Tesco allocates 1.87 percent of its pre-tax profits to charities and local community organizations.[136] Throughout its operating arena, Tesco has also focused on "computers for schools", football sponsorships, and extensive additional localized marketing to ensure it is seen as a local retailer.[137]

Tesco's international strategy is formed upon the need "to be sensitive to local expectations in other countries by entering into joint ventures with local partners, such as Samsung Group in South Korea, and Charoen Pokphand in Thailand." Tesco's international strategy also consists of appointing a high number of local personnel to management positions.[138]

Clearly, Tesco has seen the need to diversify its banners, diversify its assortment, and truly discover the local needs in each operating country. With over two thousand stores spread throughout the world, Tesco has used multiple strategies to gain market entry, including acquisitions, alliances, and joint ventures. The goal of the company is to hire local management as much as possible, but also install a number of Tesco veterans in order to help each operating area understand the Tesco guiding principles.

Key Findings:

- Tesco's fiscal 2009 sales revenue was 59.4 billion British pounds, with net income of 3.128 billion British pounds. The company operates two thousand one-hundred ninety-five stores throughout the world.

- Tesco has multiple operating formats upon which to reach customers in all geographies and countries. Tesco operates hypermarkets, supermarkets, mid-sized stores, convenience stores, and non-foods stores. Each format includes the name Tesco in its banner.

- Tesco has used multiple foreign entry modes when entering countries, including acquisition, building "ground up", joint ventures, and alliances. Each foreign entry mode is tailored to the specific market. Tesco has a 50 percent stake in Hymall in China, bought the K-Mart stores in the Czech Republic, bought the C Two stores and Fre'c to enter Japan, partnered with Sime Darby Berhad to enter Malaysia (and owns 70 percent of the operation, formed a joint venture with Samsung in South Korea (and owns 81 percent of that venture), formed a joint venture with Charoen Pokphand in Thailand (to form Tesco Lotus), and built the Fresh and Easy stores from "ground up" in the United States.

- As with each previous example of consumer goods companies, Tesco is often cited by consumer and environmental watch agencies for issues they would like to have improved, including workers' rights in Thailand and software protection in India.

- Multiple channels of customer connectivity have been the policy with Tesco from its origin. The company has a robust loyalty card program, one of the highest store brand penetrations in the world, an internet shopping experience that rivals the best competitors, and even employs its own weathermen to study past weather patterns and help place the right products in stores at the right time.

- Throughout its operations, connecting with the customer by being sensitive to local needs has been the prevailing international strategy.

Discussion Questions

1. Name four key takeaways from the Tesco case.
2. What would you do differently from the above case example?
3. Do you agree with always using the name Tesco on all banners the company acquires?
4. In the broader scheme of food retail, where does Tesco fit?
5. Who are Tesco's main competitors? Identify differentiators that could make Tesco standout against each competitor.
6. In your opinion, what are the long-term prospects for Tesco in the food industry?
7. Why do you think the Tesco expansion into the United States did not work?
8. Name two strategies and four tactics you would suggest to Tesco.

Case Nine - Carrefour

Carrefour, founded in 1957, is a pre-eminent global retailer, with headquarters in Paris, France. Carrefour is the second largest retailer in the world, behind Wal-Mart. Carrefour's operating markets are Europe, China, Colombia, Brazil, Argentina, Dominican Republic, North Africa, and other parts of Asia. Carrefour means "crossroads" in French.[139] Carrefour employs over 490,000 associates, has revenue of 87 billion Euro and operating profit of 1 billion Euro.[140]

Carrefour was founded by Marcel Fournier, Denis Defforey, and Jacques Defforey. The founders pioneered the concept of the hypermarket, a large supermarket combined with a department store. Strangely enough, but showing the impact strong retailers have on their surrounding environment, Carrefour's introduction of their private label line Produits Libres led those on the political right in France to claim that Carrefour was undermining capitalism by acclimating the population to generic foods. One author wrote that "Carrefour did more to accelerate the change to a socialist-led government in France than socialist politicians and syndicalists like Edmond Maire, Georges Marchais, Francois Mitterand, and Georges Seguy.[141]

Carrefour operates various formats throughout the world, in order to address the local needs of each operating country. Carrefour's country by country store number and format is as follows:

- ➤ China: 134 hypermarkets
- ➤ Indonesia: 37 hypermarkets, 12 supermarkets
- ➤ Bahrain: 1 hypermarket
- ➤ Japan: 7 hypermarkets
- ➤ Kuwait: 1 hypermarket
- ➤ Malaysia: 12 hypermarkets
- ➤ Oman: 2 hypermarkets
- ➤ Pakistan: 1 hypermarket
- ➤ Qatar: 3 hypermarkets
- ➤ Saudi Arabia: 11 hypermarkets
- ➤ Singapore: 2 hypermarkets
- ➤ Taiwan: 48 hypermarkets

- ➢ Thailand: 25 hypermarkets
- ➢ United Arab Emirates: 11 hypermarkets
- ➢ Morocco: 1 hypermarket
- ➢ Algeria: 2 hypermarkets, 1 supermarket
- ➢ Egypt: 5 hypermarkets
- ➢ Tunisia: 1 hypermarket, 2 supermarkets
- ➢ Belgium: 56 hypermarkets, 280 supermarkets, 257 convenience stores
- ➢ Bulgaria: 1 hypermarket
- ➢ Cyprus: 5 hypermarkets, 4 supermarkets
- ➢ France: 218 hypermarkets, 1021 supermarkets, 897 hard discounters, 3245 convenience stores, 134 cash and carry
- ➢ Greece: 28 hypermarkets, 210 supermarkets, 397 hard discounters, 216 convenience stores
- ➢ Italy: 59 hypermarkets, 485 supermarkets, 1015 convenience stores, 20 cash and carry
- ➢ Monaco: 1 supermarket
- ➢ Poland: 72 hypermarkets, 277 supermarkets, 5 convenience stores
- ➢ Portugal: 365 hard discounters
- ➢ Romania: 22 hypermarkets, 21 supermarkets,
- ➢ Russia: 5 hypermarkets
- ➢ Spain: 161 hypermarkets, 87 supermarkets, 2912 hard discounters
- ➢ Slovakia: 4 hypermarkets
- ➢ Turkey: 19 hypermarkets, 99 supermarkets, 519 hard discounters
- ➢ Argentina: 59 hypermarkets, 103 supermarkets, 395 hard discounters
- ➢ Brazil: 150 hypermarkets, 38 supermarkets, 300 hard discounters, 5 convenience stores, 34 cash and carry
- ➢ Colombia: 57 hypermarkets
- ➢ Dominican Republic: 5 hypermarkets, 10 supermarkets, 20 convenience stores, 85 cash and carry.[142]

The banners flown in each segment include:

- ➢ Hypermarkets: Carrefour, Atacadao, Hyperstar
- ➢ Supermarkets: Carrefour Bairro, Carrefour Express, Carrefour Market, Champion Mapinomovaoe, Globi, GB Supermarkets, GS, Carrefour Mini, Gima
- ➢ Hard discount: Dia, Ed, Minipreco
- ➢ Convenience stores: 5 Minutes, 8 a Huit, Marche Plus, Proxi, Sherpa, Diperdi, Smile Market, Ok!, Contact GB, GB Express, Shopi

> Cash and Carry: Promocash, Docks Market, Gross Iper[143]

The global environment allows for a scope of activity that is unlike the situation when a company only operates in one area. In one recent week, Carrefour reported that is was selling twenty Carrefour Express units in Poland, was working on a plan to cut costs by around US$ 2.6 billion, was planning to open three more hypermarkets in Romania this year, was testing a new pricing strategy in southern France, was removing all plastic bags from its stores in Spain, was sponsoring the "King of the Mountain" jersey in the upcoming Tour de France, was opening three Carrefour Express outlets in Sao Paulo, Brazil, was renovating a hypermarket in Portet-sur-Garonne for US$ 22 million, was experiencing a shipment blockage of milk in Belgium (as a demand for higher milk prices), was investing US$ 8 million in China to offer more environmentally friendly stores, and had an Israeli holding company (Koor Industries) planning to invest US$ 839 million in the company to increase its share of Carrefour to 3.03 percent.[144]

In Taiwan, where Carrefour has experienced decreasing sales, Carrefour has opened a non-hypermarket format store called Carrefour Convenient Buy. With its location in Taipei, Carrefour describes this format as a "hypermarket price, supermarket size and convenience store". The format encompasses eight-hundred sixty-five square metres and is a 24 hour operation. The format offers twenty-thousand items in its assortment and includes fresh fruit and vegetables, food, other groceries, and small appliances. With this launch, Carrefour can now work its way into smaller, less-populated areas of the island. A normal hypermarket carries around one-hundred thousand items in its assortment. This new format for Carrefour is designed to help it compete stronger against the local operator of supermarkets Pxmart.[145]

Similar to Tesco, Carrefour has adjusted its formats and banners to fit the situation in each operating country. Also similar, Carrefour has used multiple foreign entry modes to gain access to each country. With a mantra to understand the local markets first, open stores second, and continue to staff with local management, Carrefour has been widely successful in gaining market share footholds in foreign countries.

Key Findings:

- Headquartered in Paris, France, Carrefour employs over 490,000 associates worldwide, with revenue of 87 billion Euro and net operating profit of 1 billion Euro.
- Similar to Tesco, Carrefour uses multiple foreign entry modes to gain access to countries worldwide, from joint ventures to acquisitions to "ground up" building. Each entry strategy has been tailored to the specific need of the local market.
- Carrefour is credited with originally developing the hypermarket concept in the retail industry.
- As with the other global consumer goods companies and retailers, the power these companies have inside their home countries is enormous. Some have claimed that Carrefour's introduction of their store brands program led political activists to claim that Carrefour was undermining capitalism in France.
- Carrefour, similar to Tesco has multiple formats and multiple banners, in order to foster customer connectivity wherever it operates. Carrefour operates hypermarkets, supermarkets, hard discount stores, convenience stores, and cash and carries. Most banners are attempting to use some form of the Carrefour name in their banner. Banner names include Atacadao, Hyperstar, Carrefour Express, Dia, Ed, Minipreco, and Promocash.
- The complexity of operating throughout the world can be seen in one week's news that the company was selling twenty units in Poland, was on a cost-cutting move globally (US$ 2.6 billion), was opening three new hypermarkets in Romania, was experiencing a dairy strike in Belgium, and was opening new stores in Brazil.

Discussion Questions

1. Name four key takeaways from the Carrefour case.
2. What would you do differently from the above case example?
3. Do you agree with using the name Carrefour on some banners the company acquires, but not all?
4. In the broader scheme of food retail, where does Carrefour fit?
5. Who are Carrefour's main competitors? Identify differentiators that could make Carrefour standout against each competitor.
6. In your opinion, what are the long-term prospects for Carrefour in the food industry?
7. Why do you think the Carrefour expansion into the United States did not work?
8. Name two strategies and four tactics you would suggest to Carrefour.
9. What does the name Carrefour mean? Why would the company use this name?
10. If Carrefour wanted to enter the United States, what are four suggestions you would give the company?

Case Ten - Walmart

Wal-Mart, founded in 1962 by Sam Walton, is the world's largest company. With 2014 sales revenue of US$ 545 billion, and net income of US$ 18.6 billion, Wal-Mart employs over two million employees.[146] Sam Walton began his career at J.C. Penney in 1940, moved to Ben Franklin by 1942, and opened the first Wal-Mart Discount City in Rogers, Arkansas in 1962. Inside five years, the company was up to twenty-four stores, and had opened its first stores outside of Arkansas (Missouri and Oklahoma).[147] By 1975, Wal-Mart had sales of US$ 340 million and was operating in nine states.[148] By its twenty-fifth anniversary (1987), Wal-Mart had one thousand one-hundred ninety-eight stores, with US$ 16 billion in sales, and two hundred thousand employees.

In 1988, Wal-Mart opened its first Wal-Mart Supercenter, plus it opened overseas stores in Argentina and Brazil. Wal-Mart bought Asda, in the United Kingdom, in 1999 for US$ 10 billion. Wal-Mart currently controls over 25 percent of all food sales in the United States. By 2002, Wal-Mart had sales revenue of US$ 220 billion. Only three years later, Wal-Mart sales revenue was up to US$ 312 billion, with over six thousand stores throughout the world (3,800 United States, 2,800 rest of world).[149] Today, Wal-Mart operates seven thousand nine-hundred fifty-six stores, with four thousand two-hundred seventy-one located in the United States.[150]

In 2009 alone, Wal-Mart completed the following:

> ➤ January: Committed to reduce detergent phosphates by 70 percent by 2011
> ➤ February: Michael Duke became President and Chief Executive Officer
> ➤ February: Announced elimination of eight-hundred headquarter jobs
> ➤ March: Re-launched "Great Value" brand
> ➤ March: Launched "Your Zone" home décor for teens
> ➤ May: Announced newly expanded electronics departments
> ➤ June: Re-branded Marketside as "Marketside by Walmart"
> ➤ June: Opened second "Supermercado de Walmart" in Phoenix
> ➤ July: Announced Sustainable Product Index
> ➤ August: Opened "Mas Club" in Houston

Globally, Wal-Mart operates stores in the United States, Mexico, Japan, China, United Kingdom, Argentina, Brazil, Canada, Chile, Costa Rica, Guatemala, El Salvador, Nicaragua, Honduras, and Puerto Rico. Wal-Mart has had mixed results outside of North America. It has struggled for years in Japan and pulled out of Germany and South Korea. Throughout the world, Wal-Mart has kept many of the banner names from the companies it acquired: BIG, TodoDia, Mercadorama, Paiz, Nacional, Hiper Bompreco, Amigo, Maxxi, La Union, Hiper Mas, Livin, The Mall, Seiyu, Suburbia, Asda, Despensa Familiar, and la despensa de don juan. As of July, 2009, Wal-Mart's international sales were down 8 percent on last year, while the stores in the United States were up 2 percent.[151]

As the largest company in the world, Wal-Mart has the ability to single-handedly impact government policy, health care, and the livelihoods of the millions of people who are associated with the company. In 2005, then-Chief Executive Officer Lee Scott embarked on a transformation of Wal-Mart into a company known for its stewardship of the world. As Wal-Mart was suffering from a major campaign against its vendor practices, its impact on small businesses, its inability to keep the majority of its employees out of poverty, and the amount of product being sourced from overseas, Wal-Mart needed a "higher purpose."

Although it might have been received cynically by critics at first, the "green" initiative has taken hold and empowered many stakeholders to react positively. The initial intent was to spend US$ 500 million per year to raise the efficiency of its trucking fleet by 25 percent over three years and doubled within ten years. This initiative also aimed to reduce greenhouse gasses by 20 percent in seven years, cut down store energy use by 30 percent, and reduce solid waste by 25 percent from the United States stores and Sam's Clubs within three years.[152] In the process, Wal-Mart designed stores experimenting with wind turbines, photovoltaic solar panels, biofuel-capable boilers, water-cooled refrigerators, and xeriscape gardens.[153] By most accounts, Wal-Mart has served to differentiate itself in the global marketplace by focusing on lower costs and its sustainability initiative.

In attempting to connect with its customers, Wal-Mart has constantly evolved its retail banners from discount stores, to supercenters, to general merchandise stores, to restaurants, to cash and carry, to neighborhood markets, to marketside stores, and club stores. Each time a new format has been established, it has been developed to appeal to a certain type of customer or demographic. In 2007, Wal-Mart changed its slogan from "Always Low Prices. Always." to "Save Money, Live Better." This slogan change was reflective of the ability of Wal-Mart shoppers worldwide to save money, improve their lives, while also being stewards of the environment.[154]

Wal-Mart is split into three operating divisions: Wal-Mart Stores United States, Sam's Club, and Wal-Mart International.

Wal-Mart Stores United States is the largest division of the company and accounts for nearly 70 percent of annual net sales. In the United States, Wal-Mart operates discount stores, supercenters, and Neighborhood Markets. Most stores are being transformed into the preferred supercenter format or the smaller Neighborhood Markets or Marketside stores. Wal-Mart's online business, walmart.com, is also included in Wal-Mart United States.

Wal-Mart Discount Stores range in size from fifty-thousand square feet to two hundred twenty thousand square feet. These stores carry general merchandise, food pantries, garden centers, pharmacies, tire and lube centers, optical departments, photo processing, portrait studios, banks, cell phone stores, and fast food outlets. By 2008, Wal-Mart operated nine hundred seventy one discount stores.[155]

Wal-Mart Supercenters are similar to Carrefour hypermarkets, with sizes ranging from one hundred thousand square feet to over two hundred sixty thousand square feet. The Supercenters were designed to encompass the entire offering available in the Discount Stores, but also include a full-line supermarket which would offer meat, poultry, bakery, delicatessen, frozen foods, dairy products, garden produce and fresh seafood. Many Supercenters include McDonald's, Dunkin Donuts, Subway, and Blimpie. By 2008, there were two thousand four hundred forty-seven Wal-Mart Supercenters in the United States, with approximately one hundred fifty being added annually.

Wal-Mart Neighborhood Markets are regular-sized grocery stores averaging forty-two thousand square feet. The product offering includes full assortment groceries, pharmacies, health and beauty care products, photo developing, and some limited general merchandise.[156]

Wal-Mart Marketside stores are a new format of stores that are half the size of regular supermarkets, have a keener focus on fresh foods, and were opened in direct response to Tesco's Fresh and Easy stores. Even with a significant amount of stores in the United States, Wal-Mart still has many opportunities for growth, as evidenced by the fact that Wal-Mart is aggressively looking at New York City for expansion. The largest city in the United States does not have any Wal-Mart stores. Wal-Mart is looking at potential sites in the boroughs outside Manhattan, hoping to "bring a store to New York in the near future", said a company spokesperson.

Sam's Club is Wal-Mart's representation in the club format. These stores sell groceries and general merchandise, and compete directly with Costco and BJ's Wholesale. Sam's Club is a membership club, with a focus on supplying small businesses with the goods they need to operate profitably while not being large enough to operate their own distribution centers. With sales at over US$ 50 billion, Sam's is the number two volume club operator in the United States after Costco Wholesale Club.

In constantly re-inventing its customer connectivity initiatives, Sam's Club has realized the need to personalize or localize its offers to its customers. In 2008, Sam's Club launched a year-long student membership package, and lowered its membership fees for ten weeks leading up to Christmas. Sam's Club has recently opened the Mas Club, in Houston, Texas, which primarily caters to the Hispanic trade market. The store features expanded import products from Mexico, fresh produce and meats, which include a variety of cuts and a full-service meat and seafood counter. Additionally, there is a highly diverse and unique assortment of Hispanic foods and international brands across beverages, spices and sweets. The Mas Club is similar to other Sam's Clubs, because it caters to both the individual shoppers as well as small businesses. The Mas Club offers a lowered membership fee (from fifty dollars in regular clubs down to thirty-five dollars in The Mas Club) and multiple other offers which specifically cater to this demographic.[157]

Wal-Mart International is Wal-Mart's second largest division, and encompasses two thousand nine hundred eighty stores in fourteen countries. The international division accounts for roughly 20 percent of the total company's sales. Wal-Mart International operates wholly-owned divisions in Argentina, Brazil, Canada, Puerto Rico, and the United Kingdom. Wal-Mart International also operates the international stores for Sam's Club. Wal-Mart is the largest private employer in the United States and Mexico, and one of the largest in Canada.

Wal-Mart entered Canada by acquiring the Woolco division of Woolworth Canada in 1994, and currently employs over eighty thousand Canadians.[158] Wal-Mart entered the United Kingdom by buying Asda. In Canada, Wal-Mart changed the name of their stores to Wal-Mart. In the United Kingdom, Wal-Mart maintains the name Asda. As opposed to other formats, Asda is primarily a food store. Wal-Mart's Asda consists of three hundred forty stores operating under the banners of Asda Wal-Mart Supercentres, Asda Supermarkets, Asda Living, George High Street, and Asda Essentials stores.[159]

Wal-Mart has joint venture relationships in China, and many majority-owned subsidiaries (including Wal-Mex in Mexico). In Japan, Wal-Mart owns 53 percent of Seiyu. Wal-Mart also owns 51 percent of Central American Retail Holding Company (CARHCO), which consists of more than three hundred sixty supermarkets and alternate format stores in Guatemala, El Salvador, Honduras, Nicaragua, and Costa Rica.[160] To enter Brazil, Wal-Mart bought one hundred sixteen stores of the Bompreco food chain in the northeast part of the country. Two years later, Wal-Mart bought the operations of Sonae Distribution Group, taking control of Nacional and Mercadorama. Both of these supermarket chains were the leaders in the states of Rio Grande do Sul and Parana. Wal-Mart did not change the names of these stores. Wal-Mart is currently the third largest supermarket chain in Brazil, operating seventy-one Bompreco stores, twenty-seven Hiper Bompreco stores, fifteen Balaio stores, and three Hiper Magazines. Also in Brazil, Wal-Mart operates nineteen Wal-Mart Supercenters, thirteen Sam's Clubs, and two Todo Dia stores.[161]

Wal-Mart withdrew from Germany, after non-competition laws kept the company from being able to exert its size as a competitive advantage. In 2006, Wal-Mart announced a joint venture with Bharti Enterprises, so it could enter the country of India. Foreign corporations are not allowed to enter the Indian retail sector alone. In India, Wal-Mart will operate franchises and take care of the wholesale portion of the business. The operation in India requires two joint ventures for Wal-Mart.[162] In order to enter Chile, Wal-Mart acquired a controlling interest in Distribution y Servicio D&S SA.[163] On August 24, 2009, Wal-Mart reported that its Chilean subsidiary, D&S, reported second quarter and first half 2009 results of sales increasing 8.9 percent, with comparable store sales increasing 8.2 percent. Net gross profit decreased 18.9 percent during the same time period.[164]

Walmart.com was founded in 2000, and now offers more than a million items on the company website. Walmart.com carries many items not available in stores, including hot tubs and furniture. The site also offers music downloads, digital one-hour photo services, and free shipping with the "Site to Store" program. The site includes ad banners, which generate significant revenue.

Walmart logistics include one-hundred forty-seven distribution centers, and nine disaster distribution centers. The average distribution center serves seventy-five to one-hundred stores, all within a two-hundred fifty mile radius. The truck fleet of drivers covers approximately eight-hundred million miles per year. The new trucks in the system include hybrids, natural gas, and engines powered by "brown grease recycled from the in-store deli operations."[165]

Local competition and local nuances are a primary concern for any retailer operating on many fronts and in many countries. Wal-Mart is no exception. In North America, Wal-Mart's home base, Wal-Mart competes with all channels of retail. These channels include other mass (Target, Meier), superstores (Loblaw's Real Canadian Superstores), club stores (BJ's Wholesale, Costco), supermarkets (Kroger, Publix), dollar stores (Family Dollar, Dollar General), "category killers" (Toys R Us, PetSmart), and internet sites (Amazon).

In Germany, Wal-Mart could not overcome local preferences and laws, plus Aldi's 19 percent market share (Aldi's home base is located in Germany). Eight years after entering South Korea, Wal-Mart withdrew from the country and sold all of its outlets to Shinsegae, a local retailer. In China, Wal-Mart has changed its method of operating, and is working to adapt its style to Chinese preferences, like the Chinese preference for selecting their own live fish and seafood.[166] In order to merchandise properly, Wal-Mart generally places its customers into three groups:

> - Brand aspirationals: People with low incomes who are obsessed with brand names.
> - Price sensitive affluents: Wealthier shoppers who love deals.
> - Value price shoppers: People who like low prices and cannot afford much more.[167]

Wal-Mart, who normally operates in the hypermarket format in China, launched a smaller format in December, 2008. This format, called Smart Choice, operating near the Wal-Mart headquarters of Shenzen, is designed to attract budget-oriented consumers in an economic downturn. Wal-Mart is quoted as saying, "Even rich people want to save money now." Wal-Mart has also tried this format in several other markets, under the banners Super Ahorros, Bodega Express, and Changomas Express. These formats are attempting to be a smaller equivalent to Sam's Club. Inside these stores, there are only two thousand items offered, fast-movers only are carried, the décor is simple, shelf-ready packaging is a focus, and multi-pack purchases are encouraged by the pricing.[168]

In one interview with Eduardo Castro-Wright, former President of Wal-Mart North America, Wal-Mart's leadership and operating methods were discussed at length. The following is an excerpt of the interview:

Q. *What is the most important leadership lesson you've learned?*
A. Walking the talk is the most important lesson I've learned. There's nothing that destroys credibility more than not being able to look someone in the eye and have them know that they can trust you. Leadership is about trust. It's about being able to get people to go to places they never thought they could go. They can't do that if they don't trust you.
Q. *What have you learned to do more of, or less of, over time?*
A. I read something early on when I was in my first or second management role that you can accomplish almost anything in life if you do not care who takes credit for it. So I've tried to do more of that. And I've tried to do less of the things that make business more complex. I really like simplicity. At the end of the day, retailing - but you could apply this to many other businesses - is not as complicated as we would like to make it. It is pretty logical and simple, if you think about the way that you yourself would act, or do act, as a customer.
Q. *So you find that people make business more complicated than it is?*
A. No doubt about it. I think that all of us read far too many business books. I've worked 30 years now in management roles, and a number of times I've seen a new CEO come in, and the first act is typically to get the leadership team to an offsite. And you get a consultant - because you can't do it without a consultant - and the consultant then helps the team design a vision. And then you've got all these words, and several thousand dollars and a couple of days of golf later, you go back to the company to actually try to communicate that vision throughout the organization. So you hire another consultant to do that. It shouldn't be like that.

We have a very clear view of what we do for consumers around the world. And we can describe our complete strategy in 10 words. And that makes it very easy to get everybody energized and aligned.

Q. *So what do you think the process should be?*

A. I think the best source of strategy is your customer and the people who work for you. I'm not saying there's no room for a vision statement or anything like that. I'm just saying that we tend to spend too much time on that and not enough on the more practical, down-to-earth requirements that drive business.

Q. *So when you're visiting stores....*

A. I walk around the store and approach customers and ask them if they have any recommendations for us. Are there things that we're not doing that we should be doing? And I typically also will go to the back of the store. I just go mostly on my own and I get there mostly unannounced and talk to associates and ask them questions about their jobs. I ask them about their leadership in the store. I always tease them that they can tell me whether their store manager's good or bad. Almost always, you get enormous insight from those who spend their days taking care of customers.

Q. *What was the best advice you were given about your career?*

A. Someone I trusted when I was working for Nabisco convinced me that if I really wanted to have bigger and more impactful opportunities, then I probably needed to become broader in my knowledge. And I've changed industries twice since then, completely different industries.

Q. *What do you look for in job candidates?*

A. People I interview today are most likely going to be in a senior leadership role. And leadership roles in business require enormous energy - both physical and, very importantly, emotional energy. And so I try to find out whether they have the enormous amount of energy it takes to lead and manage. You're exposed so often to decisions that are emotionally charged; you have to have the balance and the energy, the emotional strength to actually do it.

Q. *What kind of questions do you ask to get at that?*

A. I ask them to share how they have dealt in the past with major issues, like a reduction in force, and major changes in the business environment. An interview is not a perfect process, right? You can't learn about people in one hour, but it is helpful.

Q. *What is your most effective time-management technique?*

A. Oh boy, time management is a work a progress, I think, for everybody in business. And if they tell you differently, then they're probably lying.

I try to get things done early in the day; things that I know are going to get in the way. Also, I have developed a system with my assistant. I send her e-mails at night. When I'm at home and I have a little bit more time and I'm more relaxed, I send very quick e-mails to her, just with things like, "Remind me tomorrow I have to do such and such thing," or, "We need to complete this or that." And I send probably 5, 6, and 10 of those that come up at night. She doesn't see them until early in the morning, but that sets the stage for the following day. And it helps me quite a bit with those things that are outside of scheduled appointments.

Q. *What would you like business schools to teach more, or less?*

A. I've done this quiz several times when we have gone to talk at business schools. I always ask people, "So who's taking accounting?" And everybody raises their hand. And, "Who's taking strategy?" And everybody raises their hand - and you go on with your typical curriculum about the business school. Mostly they are very good at teaching strategy, operations, management, finance, and accounting.

But then I ask, "O.K., how many courses have you taken on how you talk with an employee you're firing?" Or, "How do you talk with the person who comes to your office late at night to tell you that her daughter is sick and she might not be able to come in the following day?" Or, "What do you say when they come in with issues in their marriage that are impacting their job?"

As managers and leaders of people, those are the kinds of questions that one deals with probably 80 percent of the time. I think that business schools could do more to prepare kids to deal with the often more difficult side of business management and leadership. The balance of courses is probably weighted to the numeric side of business as opposed to the people side of business.

Q. *And you obviously think such things can be taught?*

A. I think they can. You can guide people to get them to understand the implications of decisions they make.

Q. *What message would you convey in a commencement speech?*

A. It would depend where, right? Here in the United States, and any of the developed countries, I would tend to provide a speech along the lines of what I said before about what makes great leaders - the fact that there's no leader who can be called one if they don't have personal integrity, or if they don't deliver results, or if they don't care about the people they lead, or if they don't have a passion for winning. At the end of the day, business is about winning.

If it were outside the United States, I probably would add something that I honestly believe - that cultural differences, which are so often touted as the rationale for making decisions in business, are grossly overrated, and that human behavior really doesn't have a language. It's pretty much the same everywhere.

We are constantly talking about differences in how consumers behave. Early on in my career, I was working in Asia, and I heard often from people about how to apply Western types of business practices to an Asian environment. But I found out, after living six years over there, that quite honestly, there were a lot more similarities to how customers behaved in Latin America, Europe and here in the U.S. than the differences everybody stressed.

So if you're training people to make exceptions for cultural differences, as opposed to following general rules, by definition you're going to be managing all the time by exceptions. And that might not be the best way to do it.[169]

Wal-Mart, as the largest company in the world, has the most complex and intense operation in any business in any sector. Entire countries do not have the Gross Domestic Product (GDP) of the company, and entire governmental agencies are focused on Wal-Mart's impact on their country. Wal-Mart is, exceedingly, one of the greatest stories of retail development in history. From the first store in 1962 to almost eight thousand stores forty-seven years later (and over US$ 400 billion in sales revenue), Wal-Mart's growth pattern has been rocket-like. Wal-Mart, similar to Tesco and Carrefour operates multiple formats and multiple banners in various countries; and has used all foreign entry methods available to gain strong-holds in marketplaces.

Key Findings:

> Wal-Mart, founded in 1962, is the world's largest company, with over US$ 400 billion in sales revenue and almost US$ 14 billion in net income. Wal-Mart employs over two million associates, while having an impact on many more millions who are related to Wal-Mart through goods or services.

> Wal-Mart has almost 100 percent household penetration in the United States, which means almost 100 percent of the American households visit Wal-Mart within a twelve month period of time. Wal-Mart sells over 20 percent of all groceries sold in the United States.

> Internationally, Wal-Mart operates in Mexico, Japan, China, the United Kingdom, Argentina, Brazil, and at least ten other countries. Wal-Mart has used acquisition, "ground up" building, joint ventures, and alliances to enter countries.

> Customer connectivity comes through multiple formats and banners and a robust website. The company operates discount stores, supercenters,

general merchandise stores, restaurants, cash and carry stores, neighborhood markets, marketside stores, and club stores.

➢ Wal-Mart splits the world into three divisions: Wal-Mart Stores United States, Sam's Club, and Wal-Mart International.

➢ The Wal-Mart Stores United States division accounts for 70 percent of total company revenue. Wal-Mart operates all formats and many banners inside the United States.

➢ Sam's Club, Wal-Mart's club store division, has over US$ 50 billion in sales revenue, but has not had much success in catching Costco. Sam's Club is constantly re-aligning its customer connectivity methods to find more ways to attract and keep customers. Sam's Club just recently opened a Hispanic-oriented club format called Mas Club.

➢ Wal-Mart International is the second largest division for Wal-Mart and accounts for 20 percent of the total company sales. Wal-Mart has wholly-owned subsidiaries in Argentina, Brazil, Canada, Puerto Rico, and the United Kingdom. Wal-Mart acquired stores to enter Canada, formed joint ventures to enter China, and built the stores "ground up" in Mexico. Wal-Mart maintains the local banner name in many markets, and has added Wal-Mart to the banner name in other markets.

➢ Wal-Mart divides its customers into: brand aspirationals, price sensitive affluents, and value price shoppers. Each customer category has a different strategy; and, sometimes, a different banner and format.

➢ Leadership at Wal-Mart worldwide is about trust and integrity. The primary mission in every store and every country can be summed in ten words. That simplicity is the key to message communication success. The company believes the best strategies come from the associates and the customers.

➢ Senior leadership is about contingency planning, expanding knowledge every day, and physical and emotional energy.

➢ The current leadership considers the differences between Eastern and Western cultures as over-stated and believes it tends to confuse what should be simple human interaction and operating guidelines.

Discussion Questions

1. Name four key takeaways from the Walmart case.
2. What would you do differently from the above case example?
3. Do you agree with Walmart's strategic outlook on how it connects with its customers?
4. In the broader scheme of food retail, where does Walmart fit?
5. Who are Walmart's main competitors? Identify differentiators that could make Walmart standout against each competitor.
6. In your opinion, what are the long-term prospects for Walmart in the food industry?
7. Why do you think Walmart's expansion into Germany did not work?
8. Name two strategies and four tactics you would suggest to Walmart.
9. What would you suggest Walmart do differently in the United States to compete against Kroger or HEB?
10. If Walmart wanted to enter Russia, what are four suggestions you would give the company?

What Have We Learned?

Customer connectivity represents a set of business processes hitting all aspects of the company. Connecting to the right customers is more than just saying the "customer is always right." Connecting means all areas of the business working together to determine just "who is the most important customer." Customer connectivity for the most important customers comes from each function pinpointing key target accounts and market segments.

Once the important customers are selected, the company's marketers must then gain a thorough knowledge of those customers' "buying influences and relevant needs."[170] The important customers can be determined by key variables such as profitability, sustainability, sales potential, or referral value.

In the examples from the cases involving Unilever, Procter and Gamble, Nestle, Kraft, InBev AB, PepsiCo, Tesco, Wal-Mart, and Carrefour, the operative success method can be summed as "know your customer." The annals of business are filled with stories of detergent company executives who never wash their clothes, oil company executives who never fill up their vehicles with gas, and bus executives who have chauffeurs drive them to work. In each of these cases, can it be said that the company's leaders are in touch with their customers? It is possible that the lower levels of the organization understand the customer, but these are not the levels that can exact sweeping changes to better the company.

In one such case, Unilever's Persil powder was recalled in 1995, after it was stated that it could "disintegrate your boxer shorts." In what was a public relations disaster, Unilever CEO Niall Fitzgerald asked thirty executives if any of them had washed their own clothes in the last six months. The answer was a unanimous "no."[171]

In order to truly understand the customer in a given market (not your *target* customer, the actual customer in the market), Davis and Dunn suggested performing Dynamic Customer Modeling. Dynamic Customer Modeling involves "analysis of customer segmentation, customer need states, customer behaviors, and influence patterns across different types of participants in a purchase process.". The modeling needs to include delving into how customers think and act within a category, make purchase decisions, use products or services, and see your brands fitting into their lives.[172]

Where the population in the United States spends 9 percent of their private consumption expenditure (PCE) on food, those in Tanzania spend 71 percent on food. In contrast, though, an average Ethiopian will consume one thousand six hundred ten calories daily (versus the recommended two thousand three-hundred) and an average citizen of the United States will consume three thousand three hundred calories per day. In low income countries, the inhabitants spend an extraordinarily high percent of their income on food, and consume about half the calories of those in first world countries. In a similar assessment, per capita dairy consumption in Africa was found to be twenty-two kilograms, consumption in Latin America to be one hundred nine kilograms, consumption in North America was two hundred seventy kilograms, and consumption in Europe was three hundred six kilograms.[173]

Knowing your customer, and then knowing what your customer is doing with your product, are two separate activities. A company is not absolved of its accountability once the product is sold to the customer. Marketing ethics have certain rules, which govern how a company should treat its customers and how the after-purchase actions by customers are just as important as pre-purchase actions.

Marketing Ethics

Is marketing a product that could potentially harm the user or others a breach of marketing ethics? Is it possible to control all possible alternate uses of a manufactured product? The major philosophical ethical theories are based upon three moral concepts: utilitarian, rights, and justice.

The *utilitarian* theories suggest that individuals should evaluate behavior in terms of its social consequence. Utilitarian theories are segregated into either *act* or *rule* utilitarian. If an individual follows act utilitarian theory, he/ she would approach business decisions solely on their outcomes or consequences. These individuals would select the act that provides the greatest social good. If he/ she were to follow the rule utilitarian theory, they would evaluate the rule under which the action falls. Following a chosen rule may not lead to the greatest benefit, but long-term use of rule utilitarian theory will lead to a greater social good. Un-ethical marketing, in a utilitarian sense, would be when a decision produces personal gain at the expense of societal gains.

The *theory of rights*, when followed, guides the user to respect the rights of individuals. These rights include the right to free consent, the right to privacy, the right to freedom of the conscience, the right to free speech, and the right to due process. The underlying tenet of this method of decision-making is one of individual freedoms, and the due respect to be given through actions.

The *theory of justice* bases all decisions on equity, fairness, and impartiality. Under these auspices, rules must be administered fairly and impartially enforced. Individuals must not be held responsible for matters over which they have no control and injured individuals should be compensated by those responsible. Additionally, people should receive differential treatment only when the basis of the treatment is related to the attainment of organizational goals.[174]

We will now relate customer connectivity and marketing ethics to a global setting in two case studies. These studies are designed to help understand the intricacies of operating in a global marketplace, and how knowing your customer and marketing ethics are ever-present variables.

Coca-Cola Case Study

Coca-Cola, the world's most recognized and valuable brand, is enjoyed by millions of consumers around the world each day. The secret formula in Coke, invented by Dr. John Pemberton in 1886, was once purported to contain cocaine as a medicinal additive. Coke is sold in nearly two hundred countries, with roughly 70 percent of the sales volume and 80 percent of its profits coming from outside the United States.[175]

Diabetes is a chronic disease that occurs when the pancreas does not produce enough insulin. Insulin regulates blood sugar. When it cannot be used, hyperglycemia (raised blood sugar) ensues. Over time, the raised blood sugar causes serious damage to many of the body's systems. In 2005, an estimated 1.1 million people died from diabetes. Almost half of diabetes deaths occur in low and middle-income countries. Diabetes is projected to increase by more than 50 percent in the next ten years.[176]

According to a Harvard's School of Public Health study, a person drinking one Coke per day gained nineteen pounds over eight years and increased their risk of developing type 2 diabetes by 83 percent.[177] India tops the list as the leading country of diabetics in the world, projected to top 30 million victims by 2020, where many towns have no insulin available or it is not affordable.[178]

To reach India's 300 million customers, Coke India has spent over US$800 million marketing to this emerging economy through advertising campaigns with film stars, using innovative promotional schemes, and famous taglines. India is considered a high priority market for Coke. The leading country for diabetic population growth in the world is also one of the top strategic growth countries for one of the leading causes of diabetes. Is Coke liable for the long-term effects of mis-use by its consumers? Can the good that Coke provides, seemingly happiness and enjoyment (considered positive effects) be over-weighed by the potential negative effects of its product?

In May, 2008, Hans Josef Brinkmann's brought suit against Coca-Cola, claiming that his diabetic condition was caused by Coke. German judge Mathias Kirsten stated, "Every consumer knows that Coke contains a not inconsiderable amount of sugar. That can be discerned from the sugary taste of the drink. It is up to the consumer to regulate his own intake of the drink."[179]

This cited example shows the inter-connectivity of the brand, the product, the customer, and the marketplace. Coca-Cola has been available for sale for over one hundred years. It is commonly known that Coke has a high volume of sugar. In this case, the judge ruled that the consumer knew what he was doing when he was drinking Coke, and that the company was not liable in his disease.

Wal-Mart and Tesco

Wal-Mart and Tesco are two of the largest companies in the world. At over US$ 500 billion in annual revenue, Wal-Mart's successes outnumber its defeats by a large margin. At over US$ 60 billion, Tesco has had similar success ratios. Sometimes, though, both companies have a tough time adapting locally when entering foreign countries. We are going to review Wal-Mart's entry into England and Tesco's entry into the United States. Both entries have had their speed bumps, and both companies have reacted differently in each example.

In a unique contrast, Wal-Mart decided to enter England to battle a "Wal-Mart-like" foe in Tesco. Tesco is the clearly dominant player in the retail sector in England. Wal-Mart's market entry strategy for England was an acquisition of ASDA Group Ltd. for US$ 10.8 billion in 1999.[180] In a normal reaction to Wal-Mart's presence, all competitors became stronger in their value offers and counter-attacked the global conqueror's presence. As within the United States, a competitor either finds a way to differentiate itself from Wal-Mart or dies trying to compete head-on. The market leader, Tesco (not one to let its market share erode) decided to exert its strong local knowledge, presence, loyalty program, and capital to fight back. In England, Wal-Mart has found itself on the receiving end of being bullied by the market leader, which is a unique juxtaposition for Wal-Mart.

Localization has simply not come easily for Wal-Mart. Some examples:

➢ Tesco, as the market leader, owns a 30 percent market share to ASDA's 17 percent, and commands operating margins in the range of 6.2 percent versus ASDA's 4.8 percent. Tesco has the upper hand in volume and can squeeze better costing from the vendors.
➢ Tesco has developed the formats to appeal to a broad base of customers, from lower to middle to upper class. ASDA primarily appeals to the lower-income shopper.
➢ Tesco has the local connections to be able to secure valuable real estate and alter its sizes to tailor to each neighborhood. ASDA primarily focuses on the Wal-Mart-like supercenters, which cannot be located in smaller geographical areas.
➢ ASDA's "everyday low prices", the strategy that has made Wal-Mart a huge success in the United States, do not resonate stronger with the English than Tesco's highly promotional pricing.

Even in an English-speaking Western country, a company from the United States that is slow to adapt to local preferences will have a difficult experience.

Now, reverse the situation. In the fall of 2007, Tesco initiated an invasion into the United States with their new Fresh and Easy concept. Their market entry strategy was to build from the "ground up", which means to find locations and build new construction rather than renovate existing buildings. The new stores were to be located in the southwestern United States, and would have a quickly executed roll-out plan.[181]

Only one year later Tesco was nearing one-hundred stores. The reviews in the industry had been soundly critical and un-forgiving. A Piper Jaffray analyst review of Fresh and Easy claimed that Tesco was "failing to attract shoppers and is missing its sales goals by 70 percent."[182]

In the first year of operation, Tesco had started, stopped, and then re-started its expansion plans, it had brought in new leadership, and was making changes in its operations. But, the company did not accept coupons, did not have a loyalty card program, forced shoppers to use self-checkout, would not meet with unions, had a fractious relationship with vendors, and did no advertising.[183] Tesco's competitors were performing these activities, which are important to American consumers.

Wal-Mart, being the market leader in the United States, did not let Tesco's entry go un-checked. Wal-Mart opened four Marketside format stores in the Phoenix, Arizona area.[184] Marketside is a directly competing format to Fresh and Easy. The Marketside stores opened with rave reviews, and complete acceptance within the industry. Is this media bias with an underlying tone of protectionism?

Having had the chance to visit the Phoenix area stores, this author was impressed with the format, execution, and effectiveness of the value offer put forth by Wal-Mart's Marketside format. We had previously visited Fresh and Easy in Las Vegas, Nevada; and then visited the Phoenix stores on the same trip. We found the stores to be sterile, un-inviting, and not offering a clear value proposition to the customer. In fact, the stores in Phoenix were offering a promotion of "$5 off a $20 purchase" during the visit. At the low margin rates in food, this type of promotion shows desperation and hopelessness. Potentially, Tesco had not listened to the actual customer base, while Wal-Mart had ensured that the customer is at the forefront of their strategy.

The above are two examples of very successful retailers entering each other's market with the audacity and hubris to think that they could be successful using their own "foreign" model of operating. Their thoughts apparently were that the format "they wanted", not necessarily the format the "customer wanted", would be successful for them. In each case, the customers have "voted with their pocketbooks" and the original financial expectations have fallen considerably short of plan. What do we learn from these examples?

- Understand your customer and cater to their unique needs and differences. If a potential country is appealing to a company, spend more time than you think is needed to research the local culture's likes and dis-likes. Follow the pattern of Yatinoo, an internet-based portal and search engine solely focused on Arabic, African, and Asian people internationally. Yatinoo is designed for these customers only and offers "tailor-made and highly targeted services, which fit users' needs and suit their special "look and feel" requirements."
- Consider joint ventures as a strong and viable method of entry into unknown or difficult markets. The joint venture, in a minority stake, allows for entry while allowing the local management to operate the business. In the case of Itochu Corporation, in order to enter China, it acquired an equity stake in Ting Hsin Holding Corporation. Ting Hsin is one of the largest Chinese food makers, and this equity method of affiliation is expected to jump-start Itochu's food operation in the Asia-Pacific region. Itochu sees the venture as a combination of Japanese quality and safety control with Chinese culture, labor, and procurement.[185]
- Follow Sheldon Habiger's five strategies for successful China entry: registration and regulations, distribution channels, exporting and entry, advertising and marketing, and knowing your customer. (Habiger, 2005)
- Take a cue from McDonald's and KFC, who realized that the Chinese acceptance of their products was dismal. They used knowledge of local culture and tradition to develop additions to the menu that included Sichuan pickle, shredded pork soup, mushroom rice, Beijing chicken rolls, and Uygur barbecue sauces.
- Factor into the operating strategy the differences between Western individualism, achievement-orientation, teamwork, and equality; and the Eastern collectivism, responsibility-orientation, conformity, non-confrontationalism, and hierarchical structure.[186]
- Spend time to understand "guanxi", and its impact on doing business in China, both from a standpoint of "getting things done" and from a balancing viewpoint between Western ideals of ethical versus un-ethical behavior. A strategy of minority interest joint venture market entry can help smooth the effects of guanxi.
- When developing a market entry strategy, consider sending expatriate managers to an education and training institute such as the Confucius Institute in Arkansas, where managers are fully-immersed in Chinese cross-cultural business relations, actions, and beliefs.[187]

- Understand your target audience, and the appropriate demographics. Those Chinese over 35 years of age still hold many of the traditional Eastern cultural beliefs of collectivism, conformity, and hierarchy. Under 35 years of age, the Generation Y Chinese have grown up in a world much more exposed to Western culture, and have begin to mix Eastern and Western cultures.[188]

- Of the four market entry strategies: acquisition, joint venture, alliance, and building "ground up", joint ventures and alliances have similarities in that they force activity that continues to refine the company's local market and cultural knowledge. These two strategies would be stronger when entering markets with cultures vastly different from the "home" culture."

- Take the lessons from Wal-Mart and Tesco, where large multi-national companies entered each other's marketplace only to learn that listening to the customer should always be the primary method to use when driving a business forward.

- Scan the environment constantly for other competitors making headway in catering to their customers, and your customers. In the case of the Wal-Mart Mas Club, this Hispanic-oriented store includes a tortilleria, a selection of Mexican-style pastries, and other ethnic offerings, including a localized butcher shop. The store signs are in Spanish, with English translations. The store also offers a more limited selection of appliances and electronics than a typical Sam's Club, offers a health clinic and a money-transfer offering. According to Kenny Folk, Sam's Club senior vice president of new business development, "We expect Mas Club to evolve as we get to know our members better. They will help us decide how fast and how far this format goes.".[189]

- In one last example, a Wal-Mart in Dearborn, Michigan has focused five hundred fifty items geared toward Arab-American shoppers. Also in this store, Wal-Mart sells Arabic music, offer Muslim greeting cards, and has thirty-five employees who speak Arabic. Twenty-two produce tables are filled with produce common in Middle Eastern dishes, and the store co-exists with local vendors by charging a dime more for a pack of pita.[190]

Clearly, market entry strategy is a driver of the future success in entering any foreign market. This strategy would consider the competitors, barriers to entry, localization needs, and cultural differences. But, a solid market entry strategy is still no match for a weak business plan. A solid business plan includes listening to, understanding, and reacting to your customers' unique and/ or changing tastes, preferences, and nuances. A solid market entry strategy cannot overcome hubris.

No strategy should involve adhering to one set of offerings, products or services, no matter the culture or country. A globalized product offering will lose out to a localized product offering every time.

Key Findings:

> If you do not have a solid business plan, no amount of customer connectivity is going to work to save the business. The plan needs to come before the marketing.

> Once you have an established plan and product, the company that works to know its customer the best will be the ultimate winner. Knowing your customer means having a business plan that is flexible enough to cross borders and change based upon customer need.

> Knowing your local "buying influences and relevant needs" is the key to global operating at the local level. You must seek to know the local customer, not your target customer. Hopefully, they will match.

> Variables, such as percent of income spent on food, and Western versus Eastern cultural nuances, will play major roles in determining the correct strategy by marketplace. The company must be flexible enough to change its business plan by local need.

> Marketing ethics can be defined through the lens of the three philosophical ethical theories of utilitarian, rights, and justice. Each of these terms focuses upon individuals' rights, respect for individuals, and equity and fairness. A company cannot just sell its product without regard for working conditions in its plants, environmental conditions in it marketplaces, and end-user issues which are the result of purchasing the product.

> Even Wal-Mart and Tesco, two of the world's largest retailers, have examples of entering foreign markets and not understanding the local needs and nuances. Both companies have more successes than failures. Sometimes success breeds hubris, which then causes a distraction from the original course of business- knowing your customer first before acting.

> Foreign entry modes joint ventures, alliances, building "ground up", and acquisitions are to be used strategically when deciding upon how to enter a market for maximum focus on ultimate success. If a market has a

tendency to be extremely complicated, intricate, and possessing a different culture, then minority stakes and alliances would be the best choices. If there are more similarities between the home market and the foreign market, then building "ground up" or acquisition would be the most effective choices.

Discussion Questions

1. Name two key takeaways from the Coca-Cola case.
2. Briefly discuss the three sides of the argument involving Coca-Cola, India, and diabetes.
3. In considering the various foreign entry models, which would be the best plan for a United States-based company entering China? How about entering Canada?
4. Relate four global operating principles to opening stores in Detroit versus Fort Lauderdale versus New York City.
5. Name two key takeaways from the case of Walmart versus Tesco.
6. What went wrong and what went right in the case of Walmart and Tesco's entrance into each other's market.
7. Name two strategies and four tactics you would suggest for Walmart's ASDA to compete against Tesco in England.
8. As Lidl expands into the United States, what four ideas would you give the company to make the expansion successful?

Global Recommendations

We will use this section to draw conclusions as to how a company and its leadership can optimally function in the global marketplace. What is the best strategic method for operating in multiple countries? According to Robert Hughes, managing director for the Middle East at Beiersdorf (owners of the Nivea brand), "It is necessary to speak to consumers, and not just to the business. It is not possible to have just one plan for all."[191] In contrast, Steve Burrows, CEO and President Anheuser Busch Asia Inc states, "Unless there are specific legal or regulatory requirements in a country, we do not alter the Budweiser recipe. It is the same worldwide."[192]

According to Perry Yeatman, vice president of brand management at Unilever Group, "The one word of advice is to be cautious and understand that there is not one answer. What will work in one culture with one brand may totally flop in another. To be truly successful, the culture and the brand are undoubtedly unique. There is little logic in trying to copy them."[193]

Which theory is correct? Due to the iconic nature of these brands, they are both correct strategies. In some cases, "one size fits all" works, and in some cases, "locally-tailored" works. The challenge is clearly centered upon the shape of the competitive environment, the marketplace being served, and the type of product being offered. In emerging markets, global brands confront low-cost local products and rapid evolution of channels. In developed markets, global brands must address the needs of aging baby boomers, ethnic population growth, and micro-marketing to ever-smaller customer segments.[194]

How does a company ensure a global brand will resonate with the consumers? Nora A. Aufreiter, David Elzinga, and Jonathan W. Gordon, in "Better Branding" suggest the use of pathway modeling. In the use of pathway modeling, a company strengthens the data used to plan and execute brand strategies and adopts statistical techniques from social sciences. With this strengthened data, marketers can develop and deliver better brand messages more quickly and precisely than ever. Pathway modeling allows marketers to determine which tangible/ intangible attributes consumers respond to and which combination of touch points can reach segments more effectively.

As an additional challenge in the global branding arena, there is a proliferation of marketing messages in the modern world. Today, people in the United States see an average of twice as many messages each day as they did in 1985.[195] With so many opportunities to communicate a brand's message, brands run the risk of falling into commoditization; as opposed to offering a unique, differentiated message to the consumer. From 1996 to 2000, the marketing costs per vehicle of the Big Three auto companies increased 87 percent, while combined market share dropped by more than 4 percentage points, representing US$ 15 billion in lost revenue in 2000 alone.[196]

In order to avoid commoditization, marketers should understand that consumers are influenced by the emotional connections they form with products. Companies should focus on all attributes of brand affiliation- the emotional relationship, the purchase process, and product attributes.

In the past, companies could provide functional benefits alone, and remain successful. Today, marketers must add an emphasis on process benefits (making transactions between buyers and sellers easier, quicker, cheaper, and more pleasant) and relationship benefits (rewarding the willingness of customers to identify themselves and to reveal their purchasing behavior).[197]

Global brands should follow four phases of active brand management:

1. **Target high-potential consumer segments-** Use market segmentation to effectively manage your resources and efforts towards the correct key consumer demographic.
2. **Isolate purchasing bottlenecks-** Identify points where the consumer would like to purchase your brand, but is turned off to the brand by various touch points, including sales people, web site ease of use, or negative word of mouth.
3. **Expand the range of consumer benefits-** Utilize an innovative selling process, promote brand interaction through relationship marketing, or appeal to the luxury or up-sell marketplace.
4. **Concentrate on consumer touch points-** Analyze and understand each point of available brand information, brand interaction, and brand word of mouth marketing that will affect purchase behavior.[198]

According to Debra Smith, vice president of communications for Retail Bank at JP Morgan Chase, "People will gravitate to a name and brand they can trust."

Ed Faruolo, vice president of marketing for CIGNA Corporation agrees, "Your brand is the one thing you own. In these times of uncertainty, people love the security of strong brands."[199]

Brand-Based Culture

A review of the successful globally-branded companies shows a common ingredient in that they have each built a brand-based culture. It is not enough to say what you aspire for your brands to mean to the consumer, the brand must be assimilated into the actions and beliefs of each of your employees. As we saw with Nestle (having over three-hundred sixty-five thousand employees), the brand must make its message resonate with each and every employee at all levels.

Why build a brand-based culture? Why not solely worry about consumers, and let the employees just "do their jobs"? The answer is the difference between "good" brands and "great" brands. With a great brand, it is obvious that the employees believe they are working for the company for a reason. Whether they ring up groceries because they are "feeding the world" or they sell vehicles because they are "saving the planet", an overall message of "why" is prevalent.

A brand-based culture:

> ➢ Provides a tangible reason for employees to believe in a company, which keeps them motivated and energized.
> ➢ Allows each employee to see how he or she fits into the grand scheme of delivering the brand vision and promise to its customers, and the effect of those efforts on the business goals.
> ➢ Develops a level of pride tied to fulfilling the brand's promise.
> ➢ Provides a great recruiting tactic as well as a powerful retention tool.
> ➢ Confirms that the customer and the brand are the things to focus upon.
> ➢ Clarifies for the employee what is on-brand and what is off-brand.[200]

In understanding the global consumer, it is suggested that grouping the consumer by lifestyle is more effective than grouping them by country of origin. What has been found, is that countries have various levels of demographics, cohorts, and consumer preferences that can sometimes be assimilated crossing country borders. Charles Taylor, from the Villanova School of Business, suggests, "The time is now for grouping consumers together, independently of their home country, into segments such as "global elite" and "global teen."

Taylor broke consumers out into four sub-segments:

> Conspicuous consumers (19 percent)- Value prestige brands with an upscale image.
> Information seekers (27 percent)- Consumers willing to put considerable effort into researching by consulting books and magazines.
> Sensation seekers (30 percent)- Consumers that value the aesthetics of their purchases.
> Utilitarian consumers (25 percent)- Consumers primarily focused upon comfort, need, and functionality.[201]

Taylor's suggestion is that lifestyle and consumption are better criteria than country, when dividing consumers by preferences.

Follow three rules for effective global marketing:

1. **Build a three-dimensional opportunity portfolio-** Create a segmentation scheme based upon the size and nature of clusters of customers who desire specific combinations of functional, process, and relationship benefits.
2. **Deliver marketing on a backbone of technology-** Properly develop the technology to "mass-customize" your customer segment offers and use data to effectively spend your marketing funds.
3. **Spend your funds where they work the hardest-** Allocate money on the basis of your customers' current and potential profitability - not revenue.[202]

Stuart Wood suggests that companies form a "tool box" of assets that "can be flexed depending upon context and content, accommodating cultural idiosyncrasies and engendering a sense of local ownership.".[203] Further adding to this suggestion, "brand assimilation" is a popular method used to bring brand consistency across global operations of multi-national companies. Brand assimilation involves utilizing education and inspiration as well as driving business process improvement through a commitment to brand-driven operationalization.[204]

It is highly recommended that a global company follow a complete analysis of its brand touch points, in order to properly align strategies and tactics by country of operation and products that cross borders. This analysis includes:

> **Pre-purchase touch points**- A collection of touch points that significantly influences whether a prospect will place your brand into his or her final purchase consideration set on the way to making a purchase.
> **Purchase touch points**- All of the brand touch points that move a customer from consideration of your brand to purchasing it.
> **Post-purchase touch points**- All of the brand touch points that are leveraged after the sale, including the actual product or service usage, to help reinforce the purchase decision.
> **Influencing touch points**- All of the brand touch points that indirectly help to make an impression of the brand on its customers and various stakeholders, such as annual reports, analysts' reports, current and past customers, and recruiting materials.

Brand assimilation "involves developing a set of activities designed to increase the probability that employees will behave in a way that is consistent with the brand over time.". By understanding how to appeal to the teens running the cash register, as well as the sales manager running the car dealership, you must understand how they each can internalize the message. For the teens, you would want to appeal to the "coolness" of being associated with your brand and the ability to convey positive word of mouth messages to other teens. For the sales manager, you must convey a message of ownership, trust, and consistency, in order to meet his/ her needs for security and job satisfaction.

The impact of each of these touch points will vary by country and product. The matrix will need to be set-up by product and country, and will include three customer types: loyal customers, one-time customers, and newer customers. Ultimately, the consumer is going to ask whether or not the brand, product, or retail outlet lived up to its promise - its value offer. Did it meet expectations? Companies need to realize that "customers are less concerned with uniqueness than with a reliable product which they know exactly what it does, and that it does it well."[205]

Follow steps to preserve market share for acquired companies in local markets, and potentially use a similar approach in both emerging and stable marketplaces:

- High income- Continue using sophisticated brand-building strategies.
- Lower income- Emulate local competitors.
- Retain the best local managers, who will likely not make major changes to the products.
- Focus on cost reduction, operational efficiency, and simplicity rather than product re-formulations or marketing efforts.
- Adhere to local standards of quality and technology. Let the consumers define quality and avoid uprooting local design and production systems.
- Acquire a local manufacturer, but keep operations separate. Share purchasing or logistics, but maintain independence in product design and pricing.[206]

As a retailer or manufacturer of consumer goods, an explicit understanding of your customer is imperative. This type of strategy has reciprocal implications. On the one hand, if your product is aspirational, and your operating country is more focused on service/ quality, then there is some re-alignment of either strategy or product to be initiated. On the other hand, if you are a deep discount retailer, and the country you are operating within primarily favors affinity marketing, then you must determine a method to attract this customer into your format or change your format.

Robert Tucker offers six suggestions in globally-operating a company and seeking sustainable value and relevance:

- Do not confuse *your* definition of value with that of your *customers*. Adding the wrong value is easy to do. When a company is so focused on its own internal processes, it sometimes forgets to ask the customer what he/ she thinks of the company's value offer. Instead of adding something that improves your value offer, you actually add something that takes value away. Interpreting customer needs can be done through customer surveys, focus groups, and one-on-one interviews.
- Figure out what business you are really in. Intelligent companies do not compete; they out-think and out-innovate the competition by adding unique value. You can only do this by understanding what business you are in. If you sell groceries, you feed people. If you rent cars, you provide transportation; and if you operate movie theatres, you provide an entertaining diversion. Understanding the value you provide to your

customers will help with out-of-the-box innovative thinking and value creation.

➤ Rethink your customers "highest need". Sometimes, you can assume the services you provide are supremely important to customers, when they actually are only part of a combination of the total value you provide. When you are so focused on completing the task at hand, you sometimes forget that the customer would still like to be addressed by name, helped out with her groceries, and provided with her "favorite" menu item without being asked. A customer still wants to feel connected and valued while enjoying the service provided.

➤ Develop new ways to listen to your customers. Use mystery shoppers, voluntary blogs, You Tube, Facebook, etc. to listen to your customers *where they are talking*. A cold, impersonal "suggestion box" is not nearly as effective as a connectivity-oriented discussion in the customer's preferred forum for communication.

➤ Brainstorm unusual ways to add value. Decrease the amount of meetings, deadlines, emergencies and other distractions that keep you from having the "free thinking time" that can lead to innovative/ entrepreneurial methods of providing value to your customers. Environmental scanning, visiting competitors, etc. leads to alternate-view creation that can then be applied to your current and future customers.

➤ Figure out the lifespan of your proposed value added service. Almost all innovation can be copied very quickly and exploited by competitors. Anticipate how long your new idea can last before being copied and de-valued by your competitors.[207]

As with businesses which only operate in one country, product connectivity in foreign countries is under the same stress. Michael Porter describes the essence of strategy formulation as "coping with competition, and that competition comes not simply from direct competitors, but from the underlying economics of the industry.". Porter's work portrayed "five forces" affecting product viability, company profitability, and customer connectivity. These five forces are as follows:

➤ Character among rival competitors: The rivalry can range from vicious to gentleman-like. The fiercer the competition, the more difficult the industry environment.

- ➢ New entry threats: The more difficult or substantial the barriers to entry, the more profitable the potential for the industry's players.
- ➢ Threat of substitute products or services: With numerous alternatives for the customers, the potential profitability declines. A monopolistic service, location, or product offering, the better the potential profitability.
- ➢ Bargaining power of suppliers: The more the suppliers have the ability to force increases in the costs of goods, and the less ability the company has to pass on these increases (the fifth force), the stronger the squeezing effect on profitability.
- ➢ Bargaining power of buyers, or customers: The increasing ability of customers to find alternatives to shopping in your store, alternatives to services you provide, or alternate solutions, the stronger the pressure on profitability.[208]

In essence, Porter's five forces and "conceptual tripod" can be combined in layman's terms, in order to understand how to offer a competitive global product locally:

- ➢ Know your customers: Without the base knowledge of your customers, and the ability to tailor your product to the individual markets, a product offering becomes generic and lacks differentiation.
- ➢ Understand the retail price sensitivity: Margin will only be maximized if you understand the retail flexibility of your product in each market. If a product is only treated as a commodity by the consumers, then profitability will be weakened.
- ➢ Watch for competitive products: Continuously keep an eye out for competitor uprisings. If your product is able to tackle a market, offer a solution to the consumer, and drive profitable sales, more than likely it will be copied very quickly by a competitor. As soon as a product is copied, the ability to price optimally decreases and the product becomes more of a commodity. This process is called "environmental scanning".
- ➢ Be entrepreneurial and passionate: Boring products are boring to consumers. A product should be marketed as light-hearted, solution-oriented, and ready to take on the world. Any other positioning leaves you vulnerable to competition.

The Boston Consulting Growth- Share Matrix is appropriate for understanding how to market each product inside its global operating environment:

> *High annual real rate of market growth and high relative market share* is labeled a "star". Everything is running smoothly in this quadrant, with product profitability growing, cash flow at neutral, and the strategy is to invest in growth.

> *High annual real rate of market growth with low relative market share* is labeled a "question mark." In this area, the product may be experiencing growth but so is the surrounding market; or, the growth may be just keeping up with the rest of the market. In this quadrant, the earnings are low, unstable, and growing, cash flow is negative, and the strategy is either to invest or divest. The products in this quadrant could become a money drain very quickly due to the competitive nature of the arena. The only way to compete and grow is through resource investment and profitability is going to be challenged.

> *Low annual real rate of market growth with high relative market share* is labeled a "cash cow". In this quadrant, earnings are high and stable, cash flow is positive, and the strategy is to "milk the cow." This strategy is not to be confused with pacifism. In this quadrant, a product will vigorously defend its market share and fend off competitors.

> *Low annual real rate of market growth with low relative market share* is labeled a "dog." In this arena, earnings are low and unstable, cash flow is neutral or negative, and the strategy is to divest. Once in this quadrant, the best choice is to get out of the business and re-focus valuable resources elsewhere.[209]

All of the companies studied, whether a retailer or a consumer goods company, followed the four control levers described by Ross Simons. The four things that must happen effectively are as follows:

> Commitment is obtained as to the purpose of the company.
> Territory is effectively "staked out".
> The job is completed.
> The company is positioned for tomorrow.

The four control levers to use in setting a common operating guide throughout the company are as follows:

> **Belief systems:** Specific sets of beliefs that define basic values, purpose, and direction. The belief systems are in place to provide momentum and guidance to potential opportunities. These belief systems can be seen in mission statements, vision statements, credos, and statements of purpose.

> **Boundary systems:** Formally-stated rules and limits tied to defined sanctions and credible threat of punishment. The boundary systems are designed to allow personal creativity within defined limits of freedom. These boundary systems can be seen in codes of conduct, strategic planning systems, asset acquisition systems, and operational systems.

> **Diagnostic control systems:** Feedback systems that monitor organizational outcomes and correct deviations from preset standards of performance. These diagnostic control systems can be seen in profit plans and budgets, goals and objectives systems, project monitoring systems, and strategic planning systems.

> **Interactive control systems:** Systems that teams use to advance and develop. These control systems are used to focus the organization on strategic uncertainties, to provoke the emergence of new initiatives and strategies, to ensure the way we do business relates very closely, and to address changes in customer needs.[210]

Building the Brand

A brand is a combination of a number of different factors. One of the most visible brand variables is the logo. The logo should reflect the power of the brand and how it connects with the end users. The logo is used as the link between the products or services offered by a company and how those products or services are perceived, valued, utilized, or otherwise benefit the end user, customer. A logo, if simple and effective, is the icon that links the brand message to the brand perception.

A logo carries the consistent message of the brand in everything it touches. Gavan Fitzsimmons, Professor of Marketing and Psychology at Duke University, stated, "Brands are almost human in representation in people's minds."[211] An effective logo is easily translated in various countries and languages.

A strong brand is worth a price premium in the eyes of both the company represented and the customer. A brand "is a promise made by a company to its customers and supported by that company."[212] The company expends extra resources in brand strategy, brand teams, and brand communication; therefore, a price premium is necessary for the gross profit returns from the brand. In the customers' eyes, the brand takes the product experience above the commodity level and makes it a unique experience to that specific brand. Therefore, the customer sees the products or services of this brand as worthy of a premium. The brand premium, on average, can command over 10 percent higher pricing than other brands in the same commodity. Some call this premium a "brand tax".

There are three strategic goals for building strong brands:

1. Increased customer loyalty
2. Competitive differentiation
3. Market leadership

Patrick Marketing Group's brand effectiveness study shows 96 percent of senior executives polled rated the "importance of brand building as either vital or important to the company's future success."[213] A powerful brand that resonates with the end-user can keep a company out of "commodity hell", where price is the only differentiator.

An additional benefit of developing a strong brand is its effect on a company's market capitalization. McKinsey analysis attributes half of the market value of the Fortune 250 companies to be tied to intangible assets, namely the value of the brand (37 percent). One study of one-hundred thirty consumer companies resulted in attributing Total Returns to Shareholders (TRS) of companies with strong brands to be 1.9 percent above industry average, and those companies with weaker brands at 3.1 percent below industry average.[214]

Once a brand is developed, and resources are allocated to its success, the most effective vehicle to promote the brand is the employee. Nothing can make or break a brand message quicker than through the various customer touch points with the company's employees. A company's brand aspirations "have to be shared by the employees and other stakeholders, not just marketing managers or even senior management. The brand is what the organization delivers, and that delivery changes almost every day for every organization that has people involved in the marketing process."[215]

Understanding the brand through the customers' eyes, while ensuring that all levels of the organization are tuned in, will sustain a brand indefinitely. The best time to build your brand is during a recession. This timing advantage is directly related to a brand's competitors. In a recession, cost reduction focus increases. It is during this time that resources should be used to prop up and build the brand, not cut costs around it. Potentially, the brand's competitors might be focusing inward and lose their brand-building drive or resources. Strong brands "generally come out of turbulent times stronger than they were before by continuing to find ways to stay relevant and remain true to their brand's promise."[216] In recessionary times, the customer also changes his/ her behavior. In uncertainty, a familiar product or service brings needed comfort to the end-user. Brand enhancements should be *increased* during recessionary times.

Which theories should be followed by companies purchasing brands in third world, emerging market, and low per capita income countries?

> ➢ Adopt the local branding and organizational strategies.
> ➢ Use local brand managers, as opposed to global brand managers. It has been found that some companies lose half of the market share of local brands when they bring in global brand managers to run successful local brands.
> ➢ Emulate your competitors. Focus on cost reduction, operational efficiency, and simplicity. Do not focus on product reformulations.
> ➢ Adhere to local standards of quality and technology. Let the consumers define quality and do not uproot local design and production systems.[217]

Keep operations separate between emerging, low per capita markets and established markets. They are different customers with different needs and wants. They cannot be easily synergized successfully. Successful branding will increase a company's cost of sales, in that a cost of sales includes resource payroll, advertising, label development, associate training, communication vehicles, and the like. A successful brand will use all of the above, and they each include costs that normally would not be present without a brand focus. It is important for a brand manager to establish a link between brand value and firm performance because:

> Like other forms of investment, expenditure on building brand value has to improve shareholder value.
> The link provides marketers the necessary justification that brand investments have the required pay-off.

The link provides for brand equity to be included in the balance sheet.[218] A brand's value is also a real number that you can value on your balance sheet. Whether it is described as goodwill in the United States, or a brand value in other developed countries, a brand is an "income producing asset"; where the income contribution can be measured and managed over time. Some believe that the brand is the most powerful asset a company owns.[219]

Take the value of the current brand, make the decision to go into the arena of diversified brand leverage, and the value of the brand expands exponentially with each successful product or service extension. A diversified brand, where the equity from the original product or service is expanded into further offerings, can earn returns to shareholders 5 percent more than average. Why does leveraging the brand add value to a company's balance sheet?

> Leveraging a brand widely tends to spread brand management support costs.
> The tendency to "convergence", in which hitherto separate industries begin to merge, means that new market opportunities are opening up in many industries.
> Relationship benefits seem to have growing importance for customers.[220]

A brand will not be a successful brand without communications playing a role that is over 50 percent of the strategy. A brand-building strategy consists of employee communication, which involves training, advertising, consensus-building, and so on. Each of these tactics is designed to build company awareness of the importance of the brand, in order to ensure each employee will likely convey a consistent message to the customers.

Customer communication will take on multiple forms, and have a heavy focus on awareness, name recognition, graphics, design, and heavy media advertising investments.[221] As with employees, a consistent message with a strong foundation is the desired outcome of customer communication. Customer communication will happen at various touch points and with various means: television/ magazine/ media advertising, in-store brand presence, product placement, word of mouth marketing, company sponsorships, social networking influence, and even airplanes that fly with messages flapping from their tail.

This chapter was designed to be a "capstone" section of the research, which is to be used in helping identify the key methods of operating which must be adhered to by any consumer goods company or retailer. Global operations take a combination of local focus, global guiding principles, a good product, solid ethical standards, and an awareness of the cultural nuances and unique variables. The research has been centered upon common business practices that can then be assimilated into a closed economic situation, which is what we will analyze in the next chapters.

Key Findings:

> "One size fits all" cannot be used in a global setting. One would argue that this mantra cannot be used in any business setting. The brand essence of products and retail banners can remain the same. Local tastes, culture, and nuance drive the end-user connectivity needed to successfully compete.

> Customers are barraged with branding messages constantly throughout the day. Your message needs to be clear, concise, and able to connect where the customer wants to connect. Depending upon the demographic, the customers may want to connect by television, iPhone, radio, or sky messages. It does not matter what you, as the business, think will connect. It matters what you discover will connect with your customers by researching your customer base.

> Targeting high potential customer segments will enable the company to spend marketing dollars efficiently and effectively. Wasting marketing funds on customers who are not compelled to listen only dilutes the message.

> A brand-based culture is one that permeates every associate and every touch point of the company. The brand exists to give purpose and meaning to the existence of the company. One must work to establish a brand before crossing geographies.

> Understand customer product usage, not just demographic or nationality. End-usage is a much higher predictor of customer success than demographic or culture.

➤ Understanding your brand touch points will make the operating plan effective. From pre-purchase to purchase to post-purchase and influencing touch points, each step of customer connectivity needs a plan and execution.

➤ It is important not to confuse *your* definition of value with that of your *customers*. You need to know the business you are really in (you do not sell televisions, you sell entertainment), understand your customer's highest need, and work to connect with your customers where they are talking.

➤ Environmental scanning is one of the most important aspects of global operating. Competitive moves, new entry threats, substitute products, supplier power, and buyer power all play into the value offer of the retailer or consumer goods company.

➤ All products and markets should be allocated inside the Boston Consulting Growth- Share Matrix. By apportioning your products or services in this manner, you can manage your profitability, control expenses, direct resources where needed, and either divest or invest in the business.

Discussion Questions

1. Name four key takeaways from this chapter.
2. Should you organize your products and merchandising around customer lifestyle or product categories? Explain your response.
3. When entering a new market, explain how "one size fits all" would be the best way to go to market.
4. When entering a new market, explain how a "locally-tailored operating model" would be the most successful operating model.
5. What is the single largest variable that impacts how your brand is conveyed to, and interpreted by, your customers. Explain.
6. Robert Tucker's six suggestions can be used globally, locally, domestically, etc. Explain how these suggestions impact how you connect with your customers.
7. Explain how Porter's Five Forces impact operating strategies.
8. Explain "the best time to build your brand is during a recession".
9. Explain the balance between cost-control in marketing your brand and optimizing customer reach and frequency.
10. What is the goal of your brand?

Example Market Analysis

Harvey's Wonderful Food Co-Op

Market Analysis
Strategies and Actions

Compiled by

Triple Eight Marketing
Integrity first, the rest will follow.
Tripleeightmarketing.com

Table of Contents

Market Analysis Purpose, Mission, Scope

Purpose

The purpose of this analysis is to analyze and synthesize the current market selling environment, while identifying key strengths- barriers to entry to be enhanced and protected, opportunities to be addressed, and external environmental threats to be reviewed for possible actions and tactical moves or alterations to the plan.

Mission

The mission of the analysis is to help Harvey's Wonderful Food Co-Op. The information is designed to assist in the further success and profitability of the co-op, and ongoing occupation of its unique niche in food retail.

Scope

The scope of the analysis is to analyze current competitors existing inside the Albany market, review all aspects of retail inside and out, and to also look at any key competitors that may have a plan to open in the market in the near future. Then, take those strengths, opportunities, and threats and aggregate them into clear and concise priorities, strategies, and actions.

Executive Summary

Harvey's Wonderful Food Co-Op (HWFC) is a retailer operating in the market that occupies a unique niche in food retail, primarily in the focus on strict product guidelines, natural and organic selection, bulk food offer, cheese and foodservice. Its members feel a sense of being part of a "club" that even the most venerable competitors do not experience.

With its unique place, HWFC has a focused and differentiated appeal to culinary experts, foodies, organic and natural casuals as well as extreme users, vegans, and all customers overtly practicing conscious capitalism in the sense of fair trade, sustainability, and environmental impact.

The following analysis will cover in great detail how HWFC is currently benchmarking versus its competitors as well as how well it is reaching its own potential, competitors or not. The analysis is broken into three main areas: strengths- barriers to entry, opportunities, and threats. We do not cover weaknesses. We believe the word "weakenesses" implies a unwillingness on behalf of the retailer to take action. It is our belief that any area that could be enhanced or improved is an opportunity. On the other end of the continuum, any strength or differentiator is a barrier to entry that sets HWFC apart from its competitors. The threats are uncontrollable external forces, which should be identified and reviewed on a quarterly basis.

The result of the analysis is that HWFC has the potential for an 8% to 10% sales increase if selective action areas are addressed and resources are applied to the areas!

Lastly, HWFC has a unique place in retail that serves as a value to its customers. With a focus on strengthening its position, and enacting a long-term plan for future power, HWFC will enjoy many more years of sales growth and ensuing profitability growth.

To summarize, Harvey's Wonderful Food Co-Op is *perfectly situated* to follow a trend in food consumption that shows no signs of leveling for quite some time. HWFC is a gem that, with the following steps added to the general strategic plan being developed, is poised for excellence. ***Greatness can be realized within HWFC's own four walls!***

Current Environment

Harvey's Wonderful Food Co-Op (HWFC) is perfectly-aligned with current and future food and lifestyle trends for the three major generations:

- Baby Boomers: Born 1946-1964, Age 50-69, 32% of population
- Generation X: Born 1965-1980, Age 34-50, 27% of population
- Millennials (Gen Y): Born after 1980, Age 18-34, 27% of population

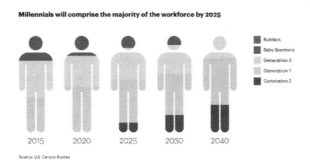

As Baby Boomers age and spending power diminishes, the next two generations will move to the forefront in societal impact. These generations have distinct impact on current and future retail trends. Overall consumer and retail trends are summarized in the following manner:

> **Formats are gone.** The massive stores are too big. All formats are shrinking. Office stores sell food, mass merchants sell natural/ organic, convenience stores sell breakfast, lunch, dinner. A contracted economy and evolving consumer has blurred all lines.
>
> **Accessibility of goods is seamless to the customer.** Ordering online, buying in-store, pick-up, delivery, drones, ordering ahead, etc. are all part of the retailer relationship.
>
> **It is more about the experience than purchasing.** Good food is sent out on Instagram, facebook, and Twitter before being consumed. Referrals from friends, reviews on Yelp, and product recommendations from friends are seen as more viable sources than advertisements or retailer-generated marketing. There are no borders between digital, social, in-store, or real life for this generation.
>
> **Everyone cares about everything.** Social, environmental, and health consciousness have moved to the forefront of purchase behavior. The Millennial generation is the first generation with a majority group that will move purchase decisions towards or away from retailers or products based upon social, environmental, or health consciousness. Included are fair trade, natural, organic, gluten free, sugar free, superberries, probiotics, waste impact, etc.

From the HWFC Mission Statement and Statements of Conscience below, there is a 100% overlap from HWFC to the Millennial generation, but not a 100% overlap from the Millennial generation to HWFC (especially in regards to format exclusivity and product accessibility). In addition, the shift from Utilitarian purchase-based in-store focus to experience-based in-store focus should be noted as a shift to be identified and fostered.

Harvey's Wonderful Food Co-Op

Mission Statement

Harvey's Wonderful is a member-owned and operated consumer cooperative that is committed to providing the community with affordable, high quality natural foods and products for healthy living. Our mission is to promote more equitable, participatory and ecologically sustainable ways of living. We welcome all who choose to participate in a community, which embraces cooperative principles, shares resources, and creates economic fairness in an atmosphere of cooperation and respect for humanity and the earth.

Statements of Conscience

- We are committed to our food policy, which reflects buying practices for food and body aids with consideration towards moral and ethical production, environmental stewardship, healthy living, and safety.
- We are committed to helping our community learn more about growing, choosing, preparing, and using natural foods.
- We are committed to learning and teaching about alternative ways of living that are healthy for ourselves, our community, and our planet.
- We are committed to encouraging an environment where ideas and philosophies can be generated, shared, and expressed freely.
- We support, embrace, and celebrate the diversity of our community.
- We are committed to providing our customers with knowledgeable staff and a positive shopping environment.
- We are committed to donating five percent (5%) of our net profits per year to local non-profit organizations.

The overlaps and the gaps between the generational trends and HWFC mission and vision identified above will be the focus of the market analysis.

Lifestyle of Health and Sustainability (LOHAS)

Now, we turn our attention to the growth of the chosen customer lifestyle track at HWFC: Lifestyle of Health and Sustainability (LOHAS). The LOHAS lifestyle is said to represent 19% of the adults in the United States and an estimated $290B in purchasing power.

LOHAS Tenets
Health
Environment
Social Justice
Personal Development
Sustainability

In each of the above tenets, HWFC has a clear representation, between natural and organic foods, nutritional products, integrated and homeopathic care (non-Rx), a robust event schedule, bulk foods, dietary supplements, and mind/ body/ spirit products. Clearly, the customer focus and alignment of HWFC was leading edge when formed in 1968. Many years of growth have been realized by the current strategy.

Among the trends from the last five years are the following, which will drive our product and assortment reviews of HWFC and its primary competitors.

Top Food Trends LOHAS Lifestyle
Produce as a differentiator
Food as fuel- protein and energy delivered wholesomely
Higher order benefits- bliss, relaxation yoga in a bottle
Leafy greens in every form- kale, watercress, spinach
Fortified waters
Chewy beverages- kombucha, live probiotics, greens
Mock meats- tofu, soybean, pea protein
Allergen free alternatives
Indulgence- nut butters, dark chocolates
South American/ African superfoods- acerola cherries, Macqui fruits, baobab
Bee-free honey
Green tea
Beets, peppers, quinoa, steel cut oatmeal
Wild versus farm-raised
Non-GMO

The trends listed in the above figure represent almost all food growth for the past five years. Projections for organic and natural food growth are seen to be over 12%

CAGR for the next three years, then leveling at 8% growth for the five years following. Organic food is estimated to represent $105B in retail sales for 2015, up from $57B in 2010. Additionally, 38% of consumers purchasing organic foods just started this behavior in the last twelve months.

Today, though, the industry has shifted from HWFC being leading edge in representing the targeted lifestyle to HWFC's being impacted by a swath of new competition. Between the opening of Whole Foods, Trader Joe's, Healthy Living Market, and the massive proliferation of LOHAS lifestyle trend products in conventional stores, HWFC is at a juncture in its connection with core customers and its ability to recruit new members into the co-op family.

If HWFC is to represent current environmental trends, considering a large existing sales base plus the impact of new competition, comparable store sales trends of +5% should be expected for the next five years. The analysis and plan that follows should allow HWFC to realize growth of 8% to 10% for the next five years upon full implementation. An average sales volume of $545,000 per non-seasonally impacted week should be the goal.

Harvey's Wonderful Food Co-Op Strengths, Opportunities, Threats

Strengths- Barriers to Entry	
• Membership advocacy	• Bulk program
• Strict product standards	• Cheese program
• Trustability	• Foodservice program
• "Club" atmosphere	• Local program
• Events	• Organic variety
• Culinary paradise	• Craft/ local beer program
• Apothecary- remedies	

Opportunities	Threats
• Name recognition	• Evolving target customers
• Seasonal program	• New entrants- format blurring, consolidation
• Produce	• Wegmans
• Bakery	• Trends
• Floral- freshness entrance	
• Deli/ Foodservice	
• Meat/ Seafood	
• Marketing- social, digital, in-store, external	
• Store brand	
• Loyalty program	
• Expansion	
• Pricing/ Dating integrity	

The *best news* in the entire analysis is that Harvey's Wonderful Food Co-Op (HWFC) possesses numerous strengths/ barriers to entry that are _completely controlled internally_. The success of HWFC will be more heavily weighted on internal actions than external impacts. HWFC already has foot traffic, a higher purpose, a pleasant shopping experience, and strong barriers to entry. These strengths are differentiators that will set HWFC apart from competitors and are primary advocacy and loyalty areas. Barriers to entry are to be protected at all costs. The goal of all key strengths is to:

- Know what makes you special
- Understand impact on customers
- Enhance protective barriers
- Communicate strengths in all brand and marketing messages

As a point, strengths are pliable and evolutionary. For example, as customers continue to evolve and new generations enter the target market, HWFC will need to evolve ahead of and with the customer. The culinary connection will be an area to cultivate going forward as cooking at home is a trend that is only building in popularity.

HWFC Strengths- Barriers to Entry

The most valuable aspect of strengths is that they are internally controlled. A mindset that strengths are barriers to entry that in turn are cultivated throughout all facets of the business should be the goal. The strengths in the previous table can be divided into *company-level* and *product-level*.

Company-level Strengths

Membership advocacy: HWFC members pay a fee to join, plus receive a discount in exchange for work inside the store. In terms of connecting employees to direct company results, the co-op format offers an intrinsic link that most large chains only wish they could incorporate. Members and employees have a reason to care and a reason to shop in the store. Strong barrier to entry to be protected, enhanced and communicated in marketing messages.
"Protect the Barrier" action: Employee expertise for customer engagement. Does this format allow for the employee knowledge and engagement evident at Whole Foods?

Strict product standards: HWFC has a product standard manual as well as a membership that has input into all products. In a sense, the strict product standards allow a "piece of mind" to be had by all customers. The analysis has shown competitors operating in the natural/ organic space to be "blurring the lines" between steadfast adherence to product standards. Multiple examples where Whole Foods, Healthy Living and Trader Joe's have a wider collection of reasons an item can be carried (Free Trade, cage-free, non-GMO, local eggs, etc.). The strict product standards at HWFC should be communicated throughout the store and in all external marketing. One discussion point should be whether the strict guidelines or member input are limiting trend identification or sales volume opportunities (rotisserie chicken, bakery items, hams for Easter, lower price point milk, etc.).
"Protect the Barrier" action: As alternate formats add HWFC-type products to a general assortment, what is the consumer trade-off between exclusive HWFC experience and "complete the shop" convenience and affordability of the other formats?

Trustability: As a result of the standards mentioned previously, the customers can trust HWFC has done their homework, understands the assortment needed for the target customer, and will ensure proper Quality Assurance is present in all levels of the business. HWFC must proactively develop and maintain an atmosphere that will allow the continuation of a trusting environment.

"Club" atmosphere: When interacting with HWFC shoppers, the store is seen as a pleasurable shopping experience where you make plans to meet your friends, feel like you are part of the "club", and truly enjoy interacting with those around you. This level of in-store experience is only enjoyed by select few merchants in food retail. "Come in, browse the offer, meet your friends, have lunch, leave feeling good about your choices" should be cultivated as a reason to join and a reason to shop HWFC.

"Protect the Barrier" action: The lifeblood of the organization is going to be how well HWFC can acquire and integrate new members and the next generation of shoppers.

Events: The event calendar allows for the extension of the HWFC brand and lifestyle. HWFC's ability to fully align the event schedule with the target customer will be paramount. Fully define the various levels of target customers and integrate lifestyle even further into the event calendar and this strength will continue to bring value.

Culinary paradise: When shopping HWFC, there is a distinct feel as a "foodies paradise" that can be cultivated and enhanced. From cooking classes to live demos to cooking utensils to groupings by recipes and ingredients, all the makings are there to allow HWFC to be a leader in all things foodie.

"Protect the Barrier" action: The connection to healthy cooking and all available ingredients and cooking ideas is somewhat under-stated at HWFC.

Product-level Strengths

Apothecary- remedies: HWFC owns one of the most extensive selections of whole health body care and apothecary products in the area. Rivaled only by Whole Foods. Shout it in all media platforms. Clearly could be a destination trip for the engaged users.

"Protect the Barrier" action: HWFC does not operate a pharmacy, like Hannaford. Having an Rx in-house "completes the connection" between self-solutions and Rx solutions.

Bulk Program: One of the top selections of bulk foods in the market. A growing trend in food, representing culinary interests, packaging concerns, healthy alternatives, etc. Bulk Foods should be seen as a the destination for all consumers.

"Protect the Barrier" action: Bulk foods are relatively under-marketed at HWFC. Why use bulk foods, how to understand categorization, representation of certain categories, etc. should be addressed.

Cheese program: A top selection in the market, with heavily engaged employees. The cheese team members offer their favorites, make a point to interact with shoppers, have product knowledge, and know their varieties. Excellent department.

"Protect the Barrier" action: Is enough being done to help in passive selling of products? Signage depicting taste, bitterness versus smooth, creamy versus non-creamy, etc. is superior at Whole Foods and Wegmans.

Foodservice program: A major source of repeat and everyday traffic at HWFC. During heavy traffic times, the seating area is over-capacity. The hot bar especially is seen as a local destination.

"Protect the Barrier" action: Whereas immediate consumption is being addressed, is enough being done for "take home" consumption? Organic rotisserie chickens, meal deals, ready to eat packs, etc. are secondary to immediate consumption but may offer a larger return if addressed. Whole Foods offers at least ten times the linear footage as HWFC, plus offers Indian, Chinese, pizza, etc.

Local program: Well represented in-store. Relationships with local farmers, dairy operators, center store purveyors, etc. is evident throughout the store.
"Protect the Barrier" action: Other competitors are catching up. All major supermarkets, plus Whole Foods and Trader Joes, offer some version of a local program. Find a way to differentiate HWFC's version of local.

Organic variety: One of the best representations in the marketplace. Truly, HWFC is a destination for organic variety. Ensure variety makes its way over to all departments, including meat, baked goods, deli, etc. Tout organic variety in all platforms.
"Protect the Barrier" action: Others are catching up. In addition to Whole Foods and Trader Joes, conventional grocery is on top of their game, especially Hannaford. One angle may be the fact that even Whole Foods "skirts the rules" at times to offer items that may or may not fit the strict product guidelines. At Whole Foods, being Fair Trade is good enough to carry an item. Healthy Living Market carries Tropicana Orange Juice and regular milk. HWFC may be the only ones left with strict all-encompassing product standards.

Craft/ Local Beer: Excellent variety and coverage of craft and local beers, including gluten free options and singles. Key product offering for the target demographic.
"Protect the Barrier" actions: Once again, the variety is matched by other traditional and non-traditional formats, including an almost identical variety at The Fresh Market and a "regular" variety on top of the craft/ local at Hannaford, Shop Rite, and Price Chopper. In addition, Price Chopper offers Growler Stations at select locales and most competitors offer a "Pick Six" mix and match section. Both are not offered at HWFC.

HWFC "Protect the Barrier" Action Checklist

o Employee expertise for customer engagement.

o Consumer trade-off between exclusive HWFC experience and "complete the shop" convenience and affordability of the other formats.

o Acquire and integrate new members and the next generation of shoppers.

o Make the connection to healthy cooking and all available ingredients and cooking ideas at HWFC.

o Having an Rx in-house "completes the connection" between self-solutions and Rx solutions.

o Marketing why use bulk foods, how to understand categorization, representation of certain categories, etc. should be addressed.

o Passive selling of cheese. Signage depicting taste, bitterness versus smooth, creamy versus non-creamy, etc. is superior at Whole Foods and Wegmans.

o Organic rotisserie chickens, meal deals, ready to eat packs, etc. are secondary to immediate consumption but may offer a larger return if addressed. Whole Foods offers at least ten times the linear footage as HWFC, plus offers Indian, Chinese, pizza, etc.

o Find a way to differentiate HWFC's version of local.

o HWFC may be the only ones left with strict all-encompassing product standards.

o Beer has an almost identical variety at The Fresh Market and a "regular" variety on top of the craft/ local at Hannaford, Shop Rite, and Price Chopper. In addition, Price Chopper offers Growler Stations at select locales and most competitors offer a "Pick Six" mix and match section. Both are not offered at HWFC.

HWFC Opportunities

Strengths- Barriers to Entry	
• Membership advocacy • Strict product standards • Trustability • "Club" atmosphere • Events • Culinary paradise • Apothecary- remedies	• Bulk program • Cheese program • Foodservice program • Local program • Organic variety • Craft/ local beer program
Opportunities	**Threats**
• Name recognition • Seasonal program • Produce • Bakery • Floral- freshness entrance • Deli/ Foodservice • Meat/ Seafood • Marketing- social, digital, in-store, external • Store brand • Loyalty program • Expansion • Pricing/ dating integrity	• Evolving target customers • New entrants- format blurring, consolidation • Wegmans • Trends

Opportunities are not weaknesses unless they are not identified nor pursued. All opportunities following are derived from competitor store visits, alternate market visits, category comparisons, and industry trends. With "Opportunities", they are ranked in order of relative scope and impact on HWFC's brand promise.

Name recognition: An informal local polling shows a clear difference between members and non-members in the actual understanding of what is offered by Harvey's Wonderful Food Co-Op. Members clearly understand the offer as natural, organic, and "good for you". Non-members had responses such as:
- o "I have no idea what they sell there."
- o "Isn't that a Weight Watchers store?"
- o "I'm not a member, so I am not allowed in that store."
- o "I am not on a weight loss program, so why should I shop there?"

The majority of the non-member responses revolved around the word "Wonderful" in the name. There was no connection made in any of those surveyed between "Harvey's Wonderful" and bulk foods. No connection. The stores that were easily connected? Whole Foods, Healthy Living Market, Trader Joes, The Fresh Market, Walmart, and Shop Rite. Learned connections (not intuitive)? Hannaford, Price Chopper, Wegmans.

Action Suggestions:
- ⇒ Start an internal group to begin the discussion of name recognition.

⇒ Determine a direction for the company. Either build and strengthen the connection, change the name, or form a tagline making the connection.
❖ High priority, especially in terms of attracting new members.
❖ Potential sales benefit: TBD

Seasonal program: The major flow of newness in food stores is based upon the consistent in-flow and out-flow of seasonal programs. The objective of seasonal programs is to be ahead of the customer before the next season hits. Being ahead reminds the customers that "this is the place to go" when the season does finally hit. Or, it prompts an urge to buy on the spot. Holiday candy, for example, will be purchased three or four times before the actual holiday hits.

In multiple visits one and two weeks before Easter, there was very little representation of Easter items, such as extra egg displays, coloring kits, Easter lilies, Easter baskets, hams, cooking trays, etc. Produce was leading with apples and cider-fall items. Easter is a major food holiday and the store needed to reflect the upcoming holiday. On top, Easter usually signifies Spring, which means cooking outside, kebabs, etc.

Action Suggestions:
⇒ Immediate formation of seasonal program, including all departments.
⇒ Map out the calendar year.
⇒ Identify key holidays and seasons.
⇒ Align product and ad in-store merchandising.
⇒ Plan for entire store makeovers as seasons and holidays approach.
⇒ Integrate all marketing media platforms, including in-store signage, social and digital.
❖ High priority, especially in consideration of incremental sales and competitive edge.
❖ Potential sales benefit: Determined by implementation energy and timeline, but could range upwards of 4% overall sales increase. Based upon current average selling volume, a seasonal program could conservatively bring an incremental $20K per week ($1M incremental sales annually).

Produce: The produce offer is a key destination spot for the majority of food shoppers, and is one of the highest-ranking considerations amongst HWFC's target market. In fact, some studies suggest produce as the top consideration of where to shop for 75% of consumers (followed by meat department and store brands). With a direct impact consideration for HWFC's target customer, this department should receive a high resource and expertise focus.

Action Suggestions:
⇒ Stadium impact in produce: start low and angle viewpoint higher as you move to the back of produce.
⇒ Sign kit with legible signs: extremely difficult signage to read, plus missing "passive selling" opportunities describing local, taste, recipes, etc.

⇒ Local message: As compared to Whole Foods, the local message is under-stated.

⇒ Baskets for sale over produce: Are they for sale, are they not? Prices? Tie-in?

⇒ Cider in March: entire seasonal make-over should happen as fruits and vegetables switch origins or seasons change.

⇒ Massive presence: very difficult to understand the sale items, "big deal" items, focus items, etc.

⇒ Green wall: should be used as a differentiator. Angle it properly, keep it fresh, communicate uses of greens. Whole Foods and Price Chopper have excellent benchmarks. Healthy Living Market does not have a green wall.

⇒ Trends: Increase visibility of latest trends- superberries, watercress, kale, spinach, red grapes, etc.

⇒ Asian presence- HWFC is in the center of a high Asian customer base, but has very little representation of Asian foods.

⇒ Peppers assortment: one of the hottest trends in food is pepper variety. Done best at Whole Foods, Wegmans, and Price Chopper.

⇒ Inconsistent produce: even on items sold by the "each", the quality is inconsistent (pineapple example).

⇒ Describe hydroponic expand in-store: excellent trend. Mention what is carried and play it up in multi-media platforms.

⇒ Massive apples as Easter approaches: Seasonality is an issue that needs to be immediately addressed.

⇒ Under assorted produce beverages: Bolthouse, Pom, Acai, Aloe, etc. Almost every fruit and vegetable is offered in a liquid form.

⇒ Tons of cider: seasonal issue for March.

⇒ Cut fruit variety: whether cut in-store or purchased cut, this section should be prominent. Whole Foods, Wegmans, Price Chopper, Shop Rite all have strong cut fruit sections. Whole Foods also has 16 linear feet of cut vegetables.

⇒ Stages of bananas: quality assurance in banana purchasing is essential. Plus, Wegmans and Whole Foods are heavy tonnage organic banana sellers, Healthy Living adds Fair Trade designation.

⇒ Organization in produce: need a planogram or flowgram. Peppers in multiple locations, tomatoes in multiple locations, etc.

⇒ Store footprint: produce may be under-sized based upon the potential of the department. If hard-wired refrigeration prevents expansion, consider auxiliary displays throughout the store.

❖ High priority considering target customer overlap.

❖ Potential sales benefit: Based upon the under-statement of meat at HWFC and the increased focus of produce by target customers, we should expect produce to have a run rate of 22% to 25% of weekly sales. Current average is 15% to 17%. Hitting expected run rate would make produce a $6.8M category for HWFC, an increase of roughly $40K per week on average store base of $505K per week. If netting 30% post-shrink profit rates, HWFC could realize an incremental annual $2M in sales and $600K net profit.

Bakery: Product considerations need to be made in the bakery. Given the dietary and nutritional guidelines, the department will require a high competency level. But, the resource allocation should show an acceptable rate if return. Natural, organic, gluten free, sprouted, etc. considerations can be found either in a thaw n serve form or baked in-store; and are available for all sub-categories (artisan bread, French bread, desserts, bagels, doughnuts, tortillas, cookies, etc.

Action Suggestions:

⇒ Form a study immediately to identify those products available to sell under strict HWFC guidelines.

⇒ Map a commodity plan for each sub-category of the bakery (artisan bread, French bread, desserts, bagels, doughnuts, tortillas, cookies, etc.).

⇒ Establish buying plan and implementation timeline.

⇒ Determine location to present a bountiful appearance in-store. One suggestion could be in front of the cheese section.

❖ High priority, based upon almost non-existent variety today.

❖ Potential sales benefit: HWFC should expect bakery to reach 3% of sales, or $787K annually. At a net gross profit of 50% post-shrink, HWFC should realize $394K net gross profit.

Floral- freshness entrance: Floral departments are freshness image setters. When located at the front of the store and merchandised for impulse purchases, floral departments set the fresh tone for the rest of the store. On average, HWFC should expect sales of $8,000 per week at a net margin of 50%. On holidays, especially Valentine's Day and Easter, the sales number could reach 10% of sales for the week, when merchandised properly.

Action Suggestions:

⇒ Form an annual plan for floral, taking into account seasonality and assortment to match the season (pointsettias, Easter lilies, Roses, bedding plants, etc. all have seasonal hits that will bring the department to life.

⇒ The front entrance and vestibule should only be floral and produce products that scream freshness and seasonal excitement!

⇒ Move the bulletin board to the hallway towards the restroom, move the seed packets, little shopping carts, anything that is not floral and produce.

❖ High priority, based upon the HWFC image and brand promise.

❖ Potential sales benefit: HWFC should expect floral sales to be double current run rates. Freshness entrance impact halo effect cannot be measured.

Deli/ Foodservice: Encompassing food consumed on-site as well as food prepared for in-home use, the deli/ foodservice area provides the greatest opportunity for repeat and multiple visits. Understanding the role of deli/ foodservice, a plan will need to be developed to address trends, newness, product tonnage, etc. The plan should be developed separating deli, breakfast, lunch, dinner, hot, cold, in-store consumed, and take-home.

Action Suggestions:

⇒ "Food type" plan to be developed for breakfast, lunch, and dinner.

⇒ Food offers to be addressed and discussed for potential to be carried at HWFC. For example, rotisserie chickens are the number one tonnage item in the majority of competitor foodservice areas. HWFC does not carry rotisserie chickens. Whole Foods and Wegmans carry organic rotisserie chickens for $13.99.

⇒ Identify full missing categories carried at competitors, such as sushi. Wegmans carries a full line of quinoa brown rice sushi. Pizza is stronger at Price Chopper and Whole Foods, while not carried at Hannaford or The Fresh Market. Wegmans has one of the most competitive sub programs in the industry.

⇒ The "power aisle" with the hot bar as the center focus could be used more optimally for increased immediate consumption items, similar to Healthy Living, Fresh Market, Whole Foods, Shop Rite, and Wegmans.

⇒ Beer is not for immediate consumption in-store, and could be moved to the back section by the cheese. The subsequent space could be used for to-go packs, increased beverages, snacks, meals to go.

⇒ Consider the value of placing a checkout in the foodservice area to be operated during peak hours and take pressure off the front-end.

⇒ Make a deli plan by lunch meats and deli salads. All major competitors have an organic selection available in the deli, with Wegmans doing the best job showcasing their offer.

⇒ Consider some type of "repeat purchase" loyalty program for continuous patrons of the foodservice area.

❖ High priority, based upon missing high tonnage categories.

❖ Potential sales benefit: TBD by commodities added (rotisserie chickens could be 10% of total foodservice sales, sushi is a target market match and is not offered at HWFC, pizza can be offered as a full program with commitment, etc.)

Meat/ Seafood: Understanding current restrictions at HWFC, it must still be stated that the majority of competitors average 22% of total store sales in meat and 4% of total store sales in seafood. At an HWFC average of 7% of total store sales, the meat and seafood departments have tremendous upside potential. If the % rate were to double, it would mean an average extra $35K per week, or $1.8M in sales annually. At 14%, HWFC would still be considerably under the regular shopping rate of customers.

Action Suggestions:

⇒ Consider the limitations as well as the upside potential and address the gaps.

⇒ Consider the "complete the shop" aspect of carrying a large portion of the plate that has not been covered previously.

❖ High priority, based upon competitor %'s as rate to sales.

❖ Potential sales benefit: Could realize between $2M to $4M incremental annual sales.

Marketing: HWFC has a great story to tell! Wholesome food, co-op, organic, bulk foods, sustainability, Fair Trade, etc. Between telling the HWFC story internally and externally, a cohesive message carrying the brand throughout all customer touchpoints is extremely important. Why shop here? What are the differentiators? How can we connect? What do we stand for? What kind of food do we carry? Why are we different? Every platform, every message, every connection with the customer should carry the same underlying message.

Action Suggestions:
- ⇒ Form a comprehensive plan describing the basic under-lying message, plus the seasonally-relevant marketing message that will be present in all aspects of customer connectivity.
- ⇒ Include in-store communication, external communication, social, digital, print, mobile, audio. All platforms have a role in communicating the message.
- ⇒ Social media: HWFC's Instagram account is well aligned with the core message. Facebook and Twitter mostly are only posting menu items with no pictures. Should be aligned.
- ⇒ In-store: Devoid of messages around social purpose, locations of sections, culinary or earth décor, etc.
- ⇒ The road communication is under-stated and confusing. What looks like the back of the store is really the main area for parking. No road sign compounds the issue.
- ⇒ Is the CDTA bus program reaching your target customer?
- ❖ High priority, mainly due to impact on current and future customer connectivity.
- ❖ Potential sales benefit: TBD, but a lack of marketing claiming your space allows other competitors to take that space.

Store brand: All competitors possess some type of three-tier store brand program (opening price point, national brand equivalent, and value-added tier). HWFC has a limited assortment, primarily in the vitamin and supplement section. The benefits of a store brand program include repeat purchases, store loyalty, in-house advertising, value message, and margin enhancement.

Action Suggestions:
- ⇒ Form a plan for a store brand procurement source, whether a consolidator or a wholesaler. More than likely, the volume minimums will not be attainable by HWFC alone.
- ⇒ Decide the tiers needed and number of sku's possible.
- ⇒ Form timeline and implementation plan.
- ❖ Medium priority, based upon benefit enhancement. Effort will be high.
- ❖ Potential sales benefit: TBD, determined by number of sku's, departments, sourcing, etc. Most retailers aim for a 25% store brand penetration with an average of 10% higher margin rate. Could mean $650,000 incremental net margin, not counting qualitative benefits.

Loyalty program: The future of retailing lies in the use of big data in order to personalize the customer engagement. In essence, the retailer trades a customer discount in exchange for the customer's data. The data is then used to enhance the relationship as well as efficiently and effectively the marketing funds. Except for Fresh Market, Whole Foods, and Healthy Living, all competitors have a loyalty card.

<u>Action Suggestions:</u>
- ⇒ Decide if HWFC has the resources and desire to pursue the opportunity.
- ⇒ If yes, develop the plan.
- ❖ Medium priority, as some data collection can happen "generically" as opposed to customer-specific, and can still be used to promote complementary items.
- ❖ Potential sales benefit: TBD

Expansion: Inevitably, aggregated volume would be a stronger future position for HWFC than a sole unit. But, expansion would be its own plan, to include target market, real estate direction, best fit, acquire or build ground-up, continued synergies of fixed costs (including advertising and media), etc.

<u>Action Suggestions:</u>
- ⇒ Decide upon necessity of expansion.
- ⇒ Determine financial impact and viability.
- ⇒ In the market, it has been heard that Healthy Living in Saratoga is for sale. Recommendation is not to buy, based upon mall location. Investigation in-store and externally reveals a strong disappointment by Healthy Living in their current results, which is forcing them to go into "shrink control" mode as well as diluting their brand (carrying mainstream items just for tonnage).
- ⇒ Between Clifton Park and Saratoga would be the most natural target market match for HWFC.
- ⇒ We do not know of any Wegmans plans at this time, but they are probably the most secretive of any retailer for Albany plans.
- ⇒ Whole Foods, Fresh Market, and Trader Joe's could easily open at least one more store in the Saratoga area.
- ⇒ Price Chopper is re-branding to Market 32, which includes a heavier collection of natural and organic, as well it will build customer buzz and interest.
- ⇒ Shop Rite is satisfied with half their results (Niskayuna and Central Avenue) and would like to see improved results at their other two stores (Colonie and Slingerlands).
- ⇒ Hannaford is only remodeling in Albany, with no public plans for new sites.
- ⇒ One competitor to watch, and it is a perfect overlap for customers, is Adams out of the Downstate area. Showing double digit growth in their three stores, and Albany would be a natural expansion area.
- ⇒ No expansion plans into Albany for Ahold.
- ⇒ Kroger is a continuous rumor for northeast expansion, although it is not known if Albany area would be first (unless they acquire).

Pricing/ dating integrity: Multiple examples of line families of brands with varying retail prices, as well out of date items on the shelf and product rotation needs. These two issues are the basics of running the operation, have multiple margin and customer confidence impacts, and could lead to health issues if out of date product is sold.

Action Suggestions:

⇒ Immediate implementation and training of product rotation plan, focusing on key areas first (dairy).

⇒ Review and implementation of pricing program, to link like sku's, ensure price changes are completed in a timely manner and reflect all cost increases through retail changes immediately, for margin enhancement or control.

HWFC Opportunities Action Checklist

- Start an internal group to begin the discussion of name recognition.
- Determine a direction for the company. Either build and strengthen the connection, change the name, or form a tagline making the connection.
- Immediate formation of seasonal program, including all departments.
- Map out the calendar year.
- Identify key holidays and seasons.
- Align product and ad in-store merchandising.
- Plan for entire store makeovers as seasons and holidays approach.
- Integrate all marketing media platforms, including in-store signage, social and digital.
- Stadium impact in produce: start low and angle viewpoint higher as you move to the back of produce.
- Sign kit with legible signs: extremely difficult signage to read, plus missing "passive selling" opportunities describing local, taste, recipes, etc.
- Local message: As compared to Whole Foods, the local message is under-stated.
- Baskets for sale over produce: Are they for sale, are they not? Prices? Tie-in?
- Cider in March: entire seasonal make-over should happen as fruits and vegetables switch origins or seasons change.
- Massive presence: very difficult to understand the sale items, "big deal" items, focus items, etc.
- Green wall: should be used as a differentiator. Angle it properly, keep it fresh, communicate uses of greens. Whole Foods and Price Chopper have excellent benchmarks. Healthy Living Market does not have a green wall.
- Trends: Increase visibility of latest trends- superberries, watercress, kale, spinach, red grapes, etc.
- Asian presence- HWFC is in the center of a high Asian customer base, but has very little representation of Asian foods.
- Peppers assortment: one of the hottest trends in food is pepper variety. Done best at Whole Foods, Wegmans, and Price Chopper.
- Inconsistent produce: even on items sold by the "each", the quality is inconsistent (pineapple example).
- Describe hydroponic expand in-store: excellent trend. Mention what is carried and play it up in multi-media platforms.
- Massive apples as Easter approaches: Seasonality is an issue that needs to be immediately addressed.
- Under assorted produce beverages: Bolthouse, Pom, Acai, Aloe, etc. Almost every fruit and vegetable is offered in a liquid form.
- Tons of cider: seasonal issue for March.
- Cut fruit variety: whether cut in-store or purchased cut, this section should be prominent. Whole Foods, Wegmans, Price Chopper, Shop Rite all have strong cut fruit sections. Whole Foods also has 16 linear feet of cut vegetables.

- Stages of bananas: quality assurance in banana purchasing is essential. Plus, Wegmans and Whole Foods are heavy tonnage organic banana sellers, Healthy Living adds Fair Trade designation.
- Organization in produce: need a planogram or flowgram. Peppers in multiple locations, tomatoes in multiple locations, etc.
- Store footprint: produce may be under-sized based upon the potential of the department. If hard-wired refrigeration prevents expansion, consider auxiliary displays throughout the store.
- Form a study immediately to identify those products available to sell under strict HWFC guidelines.
- Map a commodity plan for each sub-category of the bakery (artisan bread, French bread, desserts, bagels, doughnuts, tortillas, cookies, etc.).
- Establish buying plan and implementation timeline.
- Determine location to present a bountiful appearance in-store. One suggestion could be in front of the cheese section.
- Form an annual plan for floral, taking into account seasonality and assortment to match the season (pointsettias, Easter lilies, Roses, bedding plants, etc. all have seasonal hits that will bring the department to life.
- The front entrance and vestibule should only be floral and produce products that scream freshness and seasonal excitement!
- Move the bulletin board to the hallway towards the restroom, move the seed packets, little shopping carts, anything that is not floral and produce.
- "Food type" plan to be developed for breakfast, lunch, and dinner.
- Food offers to be addressed and discussed for potential to be carried at HWFC. For example, rotisserie chickens are the number one tonnage item in the majority of competitor foodservice areas. HWFC does not carry rotisserie chickens. Whole Foods and Wegmans carry organic rotisserie chickens for $13.99.
- Identify full missing categories carried at competitors, such as sushi. Wegmans carries a full line of quinoa brown rice sushi. Pizza is stronger at Price Chopper and Whole Foods, while not carried at Hannaford or The Fresh Market. Wegmans has one of the most competitive sub programs in the industry.
- The "power aisle" with the hot bar as the center focus could be used more optimally for increased immediate consumption items, similar to Healthy Living, Fresh Market, Whole Foods, Shop Rite, and Wegmans.
- Beer is not for immediate consumption in-store, and could be moved to the back section by the cheese. The subsequent space could be used for to-go packs, increased beverages, snacks, meals to go.
- Consider the value of placing a checkout in the foodservice area to be operated during peak hours and take pressure off the front-end.
- Make a deli plan by lunch meats and deli salads. All major competitors have an organic selection available in the deli, with Wegmans doing the best job showcasing their offer.

- Consider some type of "repeat purchase" loyalty program for continuous patrons of the foodservice area.
- Consider the limitations as well as the upside potential and address the gaps.
- Consider the "complete the shop" aspect of carrying a large portion of the plate that has not been covered previously.
- Form a comprehensive plan describing the basic under-lying message, plus the seasonally-relevant marketing message that will be present in all aspects of customer connectivity.
- Include in-store communication, external communication, social, digital, print, mobile, audio. All platforms have a role in communicating the message.
- Social media: HWFC's Instagram account is well aligned with the core message. Facebook and Twitter mostly are only posting menu items with no pictures. Should be aligned.
- In-store: Devoid of messages around social purpose, locations of sections, culinary or earth décor, etc.
- The road communication is under-stated and confusing. What looks like the back of the store is really the main area for parking. No road sign compounds the issue.
- Is the CDTA bus program reaching your target customer?
- Form a plan for a store brand procurement source, whether a consolidator or a wholesaler. More than likely, the volume minimums will not be attainable by HWFC alone.
- Decide the tiers needed and number of sku's possible.
- Form timeline and implementation plan.
- Decide if HWFC has the resources and desire to pursue the opportunity.
- If yes, develop the plan.
- Decide upon necessity of expansion.
- Determine financial impact and viability.
- In the market, it has been heard that Healthy Living in Saratoga is for sale. Recommendation is not to buy, based upon mall location. Investigation in-store and externally reveals a strong disappointment by Healthy Living in their current results, which is forcing them to go into "shrink control" mode as well as diluting their brand (carrying mainstream items just for tonnage).
- Between Clifton Park and Saratoga would be the most natural target market match for HWFC.
- We do not know of any Wegmans plans at this time, but they are probably the most secretive of any retailer for Albany plans.
- Whole Foods, Fresh Market, and Trader Joe's could easily open at least one more store in the Saratoga area.
- Price Chopper is re-branding to Market 32, which includes a heavier collection of natural and organic, as well it will build customer buzz and interest.
- Shop Rite is satisfied with half their results (Niskayuna and Central Avenue) and would like to see improved results at their other two stores (Colonie and Slingerlands).

- Hannaford is only remodeling in Albany, with no public plans for new sites.
- One competitor to watch, and it is a perfect overlap for customers, is Adams out of the Downstate area. Showing double digit growth in their three stores, and Albany would be a natural expansion area.
- No expansion plans into Albany for Ahold.
- Kroger is a continuous rumor for northeast expansion, although it is not known if Albany area would be first (unless they acquire).
- Immediate implementation and training of product rotation plan, focusing on key areas first (dairy).
- Review and implementation of pricing program, to link like sku's, ensure price changes are completed in a timely manner and reflect all cost increases through retail changes immediately, for margin enhancement or control.

HWFC Threats

Strengths- Barriers to Entry	
• Membership advocacy • Strict product standards • Trustability • "Club" atmosphere • Events • Culinary Paradise • Apothecary- remedies	• Bulk program • Cheese program • Foodservice program • Local program • Organic variety • Craft/ local beer variety
Opportunities	**Threats**
• Name recognition • Seasonal program • Produce • Bakery • Floral- freshness entrance • Deli/ Foodservice • Meat/ Seafood • Marketing- social, digital, in-store, external • Store brand • Loyalty program • Expansion • Pricing/ dating integrity	• Evolving customers • New entrants- format blurring, consolidation • Wegmans • Trends

Threats to HWFC, in this study, can be defined as those external threats against which there is very little control. The best solution is to remain aware of the identified threats and place internal focus to ensure the threats are reviewed on a quarterly basis. You cannot alter the threat, but you can always position HWFC to accentuate barriers to entry and mitigate threat impacts.

Evolving customers: The natural and organic customer is evolving as the next generation gains more buying power. From being a "fringe" of the population, today's natural and organic customer is becoming more mainstream and more overall socially conscious. The data shows health and wellness will remain on its current strong trend for the undeterminable future. Added to that trend will be sustainability, social consciousness, a desire to spend less and less on everything, and a desire to be socially and digitally connected to their retailers. There is a certain platform agnosticism that forces the need to discuss online ordering and delivery/ pick-up, in-store mobile deals, endless aisles online, extreme personalization, etc. Be assured, though, all parties must be onboard before embarking into online ordering for delivery or pick-up.

New entrants- format blurring, consolidation: With the aforementioned growth in attractiveness for natural and organic products, all retailers are entering the market in some manner. From "pure play" retailers like Whole Foods to "complete shop" retailers like Hannaford, Shop Rite, and Price Chopper to "mass merchant" retailers like Walmart and Target, all formats are seeing the benefit of carrying more food and more natural and organic food as well. Pallets of Ella's Kitchen baby food are available at Walmart, along with over 120 Wild Oats organic items. Aldi has a complete branded gluten-free line. With this blurring of channels, HWFC will see the benefit of discussing how well it can maintain its rigid product guidelines while all other formats are adding item after item that was once only found at HWFC.

Wegmans: A Wegmans entry into the Albany market would be a game changer for all area retailers. They are the number-one voted supermarket in the country year after year, have one of the widest selections of natural and organic of any competitors, and offer the customer the ability to complete the shop with extensive foodservice, competitive center store prices, club packs, and high customer engagement. On top, the other retailers' reactions to Wegmans would bring the competitive environment to a fever pitch.

Trends: As soon as superberries are the rage, along comes kale. As soon as kale is integrated into every form of food possible, along comes watercress, or ancient grains, or quinoa, or spinach, or detox, etc. Trends in food are happening at a lightning pace. HWFC will need to ensure there is a "watchdog" to identify and cover trends as they happen or even before they happen. HWFC's niche is only accentuated when a trend is identified and covered in HWFC first.

Conclusion

Harvey's Wonderful Food Co-Op is perfectly aligned with the trends and growth in food for now and into the future. As with all positive trends though, competitors are aiming to participate as well. The good news is that HWFC could see an 8% to 10% sales increase by enacting the above in-store actions! There is a tremendous amount of potential right at your fingertips. The above analysis and action points have been designed to format a strategy and plan around prioritized strengths and opportunities, along with a keen eye on uncontrollable threats.

HWFC will be strong even if none of the above items are acted upon. But, enacted and implemented....the sky is the limit!

Triple Eight Marketing
Integrity first, the rest will follow.
Tripleeightmarketing.com

Theoretical Framework

Introduction

Global brands and retailers face similar challenges when moving into countries or areas outside of their home base. The customer complexion that made the retailer or consumer brand successful in its originating country or city changes as each subsequent border is crossed. The question of what strategy to follow while entering new markets, from a branding standpoint, is a balance between aggregated synergies from common elements in each brand versus the localization needed to ensure a brand's success.

Many customers in the global marketplace are saying they want more from a brand or retailer. No longer is it acceptable to offer a "one size fits all" approach to brand presence, store layout, and consumer marketing interaction. Customers would like to be recognized as individuals, where each person feels a connection to the larger make-up of the brand or store banner. They demand personal service, to be connected to your brand where *they* want to be connected (where they are receptive to messages), and a brand or shopping experience that resonates with their emotions and feelings of ownership to the brand or store.

When you add in the variable of operating in a *closed* economic society, the intricacy of running a global business increases exponentially.

The quandary for a global consumer good company or retailer revolves around a few formative questions:

➢ How do we connect with the local customers in each operating country?
➢ How can we form a strategy entailing a local approach, while benefiting from the global scale of the company?
➢ What type of consumer research is needed to form brand connection and consumer retention strategies?
➢ Can countries be grouped by similar characteristics, in order to facilitate the need for a strategy formation country by country?
➢ Which format for connectivity (digital, social, print, billboards, etc.) resonates the strongest with our target customer?

➢ What are the common practices used by other brands and retailers, which can be used for our own strategy formulation?

Statement of the Problem

The reasons to pursue strategic growth are many: more customers, increased revenue, emerging markets, and global synergies and scale. Unfortunately for consumer goods companies and retailers, the goals of expansion are sometimes counter-effecting:

➢ In order to be a successful retailer or brand, the brand essence must resonate with the local customers. A specific marketing plan country by country can be the most effective method of operating.
➢ In order to affect global scale and synergies, a certain amount of consistency must be attained. A specific marketing plan country by country can be costly and inefficient.

The question of customer connectivity and emotional resonance also plays a major part in the final strategy recommendations:

➢ How do customers in various countries want to receive marketing communication?
➢ How do you balance the need to communicate efficiently and effectively with the consumer's need to receive a personalized message that is customer and country-specific?

Purpose of the Study

In this research, we analyzed the most effective strategies for global brands and retailers, taking into account the balanced need for synergies and scale versus localization and customer marketing interaction. The paradoxical relationship between these factors belies the need to investigate best practices, case studies, surveys of top global companies, and other research so that an effective strategy for global marketing of consumer goods products and retailers can be formulated.

The analysis involved normal key performance indicator success points (net operating profits, sales), as well as assumptions gathered through qualitative and sources within the targeted companies.

Among the companies analyzed were: Nestle SA, Procter and Gamble, InBev AB, Unilever, Kraft, PepsiCo/ Frito-Lay, Tesco, Carrefour, and Wal-Mart.

The methods of customer communication analyzed included: in-store branding, print media, electronic communication, viral messaging, word of mouth messaging, television, billboard marketing, and other social media.

Questions and/ or Hypotheses

The specific research goal was focused upon the belief that, in order for a brand or retailer to be successful, the customer must be at the center of their marketing strategy; and how this can happen when global scale and efficiencies must be paired with localization. Additionally, which method of communicating with the customers is the most effective country by country? Do some areas of the world prefer different types of communication than other areas?

The Design- Methods and Procedures

The design of the research was as follows:

- ➢ Initial research into existing studies and conclusions.
- ➢ Developed a formulation of in-depth surveys that were covered in-person or electronically with key leaders within the targeted companies.
- ➢ Complete research of global marketing strategies, nuances, and methods of doing business.
- ➢ Researched and compiled net operating earnings and sales revenue of each of the targeted companies, using country-specific results if available. If they were not available, made assumptions based upon expansion activity; where increased expansion would be correlated with positive results in a specific country.
- ➢ Researched the various country-specific nuances and cultural orientations, which affect spending patterns in that country.
- ➢ Researched various methods of communication media, and theories of customer connectivity.
- ➢ Compiled a list of communication methods used by the targeted companies from surveys or interviews.
- ➢ Completed an analysis of all collected variables in order to derive conclusive evidence to be used for strategy formulation.

The confounding variables to be controlled included country-specific economic status and growth, inflationary effects, war effects, market entry strategies, and cultural effects. Each of these variables could impact results, and were to be controlled through normalization, awareness, and factoring into the analysis.

The random variables were the sales and revenue results, the media communication methods, and the global marketing strategies employed by each of the targeted companies.

Sampling

The targeted companies embodied a representative sample matched by these common variables:

- The companies all had operations in at least twenty countries.
- The companies all had operations in both eastern and western cultures.
- The companies studied were all undergoing continued expansion.
- The companies all had a standing in the "Top Five" of their operating sector or segment.
- The companies were all using multiple choices of media.
- The companies all possessed varied market entry strategies and expansion outlooks.

Instrumentation

The instruments used to collect company data were primarily surveys and research obtained either in person, or electronically. The survey questions, generally, were as follows:

- How do global companies handle the various cultural differences across borders?
- Do you have a specific means of sharing local values with expatriates you send to various countries?
- Do you value or participate in bringing inpatriates into the existing global management team?
- Do you have different strategies for emerging versus established countries?

- When you enter a country, is the ability to work with and possibly assimilate the existing cultures a consideration?
- Is the business opportunity the primary consideration?
- How do you determine when a brand's traits should be locally altered or kept consistent in all markets?
- In what way have you adapted brands to emerging economies versus established economies?
- Is per capita income a consideration when deciding upon adapting or changing a brand strategy?
- How do you monetize, or gauge the return on viral marketing and social networking strategies?
- Do you have a strategy for viral marketing/ social networking?
- How do you determine how you will connect with each demographic cohort?
- What is your primary data source in determining brand positioning in each country?
- What steps have you taken to offer a locally relevant brand, while gaining the needed synergies of a global company?

Data Collection

The financial and directional data was collected through intensive research of the targeted companies' financial statements and available public documents. The country-specific operating and cultural data was collected through document research.

The survey data was collected either through an electronic means or by in-person interviews. The timing of the survey data began immediately with the first contact of the targeted companies and formation of a relationship.

Data Analysis

Upon collection of the research data and survey results, each company's information was appropriately compared with other targeted companies.

Financial data was used to determine the by-country success of the targeted companies. The attributes were prioritized in the following manner: sales and revenue, net gross profit, expansion plans, operating countries, global expansion strategies, marketing medium preferences, number of global products, and number of global banners.

The rationale behind using surveys coupled with research was that correlative relationships between global marketing strategies and their success was the most effective method to draw conclusions from data.

Limitations and Delimitations

A potential limitation of this study was the qualitative nature of the data. It was believed, though, qualitative mixed with quantitative was the most effect tive and efficient available method upon which to draw conclusions to the question of global marketing strategies.

As a de-limitation, we only studied companies that were primarily English-speaking (except Carrefour) in their home country. They were all facing similar challenges in operating from a western-based culture and nature. They were all facing similar challenges in taking a western operation into the global marketplace.

Significance of the Study

As a company based in a western culture, and espousing the need for globalization, much can be learned from peer or competitive companies in how certain go-to-market strategies have proven successful. We expected to find anomalies that did not correlate, but delineated the underlying success points from the targeted companies and formed them into a successful global marketing business plan that can be used by any company in the future.

The information gathered and the plan developed could prove invaluable for future goal-setting for practitioners in the retail/ consumer goods world. For scholars, this research approach would prove challenging and rewarding, in that multiple variables may or may not correlate; but the resulting global marketing plan will be developed using the most effective and efficient available research and analysis. Data obtained from rival companies that normally do not share their best practices will benefit both practitioners and scholars.

A "blueprint for success", developed with extensive research from literature, financial results, and survey responses, could prove invaluable to companies involved in global expansion, especially in closed or transitioning economic societies.

Recommendations

For practicing business people, the question of global marketing strategies, as well as marketing mode choices, resonates highly. The variables of the different commodities, as well as countries being served, could help in determining a simplified approach to market entry. As a result, resources spent on ineffective entry methods or operating strategies can be saved by progressive global companies.

Bibliography

Abreu Filho, Gilberto Duarte de; Calicchio, Nicola; Lunardini, Fernando. (2003). Brand Building in Emerging Markets. *The McKinsey Quarterly.* 2003 Special Edition: The Value in Organization. pp. 6-9.

Ackerman, Elise. (2008). eBay Tops Analysts' Estimates. *McClatchy- Tribune Business News.* Retrieved ProQuest: November 21, 2008. ProQuest document ID: 1464024231.

Alon, Ilon. (2004). International Market Selection for a Small Enterprise: A Case Study in International Entrepreneurship. *SAM Advanced Management Journal.* 69(1).

Aisner, James. (2000). Global Brands: Connecting With Consumers Across Boundaries. *Harvard Business School Working Knowledge.* pp. 1-4. Retrieved May 16, 2008. http://hbswk.hbs.edu/item/1621.html.

Anheuser-Busch personal interview with Steve Burrows, CEO and President Anheuser-Busch Asia Inc. May 12, 2008.

Anonymous. (2004). Coca-Cola India in 2004- Marketing Strategy. *ICM Center for Management.* Retrieved: January 20, 2009. www.icmrindia.org.

Anonymous. (2008). Itochu Announces Investment in Major China Food Maker. *Jiji Press English News Service.* Retrieved ProQuest: November 21, 2008. ProQuest document ID: 1598796521.

Anonymous. (2008). Karina's Kolumn. *The Banker.* pp. 1-3. Retrieved ProQuest: May 16, 2008. ProQuest document ID: 1471488731.

Anonymous. (2005). P&G Groomed for Global Dominance: Gillette Strives for Cutting-Edge Expertise. *Strategic Direction.* 21(10). pp. 12-15. Retrieved ProQuest: May 16, 2008. ProQuest document ID: 928560381.

Anonymous. (2009). German Blames Coke for Diabetes. *The Financial Express.* Retrieved: January 20, 2009. www.financialexpress.com.
Anonymous. (2008). The Four Levers of Control. *Career Development Plan.* Retrieved: July 7, 2008. www.careerdevelopmentplan.net.

Anonymous. (2008). Yatinoo Announces International Expansion Strategy and Positions Itself in Contrast to Google, Yahoo, EBay, and Others. *PR Newswire.* Retrieved ProQuest: November 21, 2008. ProQuest document ID: 1581152811.

Anonymous Personal Interview. (2009). Interview with anonymous person serving as Chief Operating Officer of the un-disclosed company. August 4, 2009.

Antoncic, Bostjan; Hisrich, Robert. (2003). Privatization, Corporate Entrepreneurship, and Performance: Testing a Normative Model. *Journal of Developmental Entrepreneurship.* 8(3).

Apps, Peter. (2007). Backing Business in Africa. *Alertnet.* Retrieved: August 3, 2009. www.alertnet.org.

Argandona, Antonio. (2004). On Ethical, Social, and Environmental Management Systems. *Journal of Business Ethics.* 51(1).

Asda. (2007). Customer Services Asda: Frequently Asked Questions. *Asda.* November 1, 2007. Retrieved: June 8, 2009. www.wikipedia.org.

Attwood, James. (2009). Wal-Mart Completes Takeover of Chilean Grocer D&S. *Bloomberg.* www.bloomberg.com. January 23, 2009. Retrieved: June 8, 2009. www.wikipedia.org.

Auto News. (2007). Global Brands Suffer Power Drain According to GFK Roper Consulting Annual Worldwide....*Auto News.* pg. 1. Retrieved May 16, 2008. http://www.automotive.com/auto-news/02/30592/index.html.

Balfour, Frederick. (2006). TOM Online: eBay's Last China Card. *Business Week (Online).* Retrieved ProQuest: November 21, 2008. ProQuest document ID: 1183368161.

Ball, Deborah. (2007). After Buying Binge, Nestle Goes on a Diet; Departing CEO Slashes Slow Sellers, Brands; "No" to Low-Carb Rolo. *Wall Street Journal.* pp. 1-5. Retrieved ProQuest: May 16, 2008. http://proquest.umi.com.

Balwani, Samir. (2009). 5 Easy Social Media Wins for your Small Business. *Mashable.com.* Retrieved: August 21, 2009. www.mashable.com.

Barbaro, Michael. (2007). It's Not Only About Price At Wal-Mart. *New York Times.* March 2, 2007. Retrieved: June 8, 2009. www.wikiepdia.org.

Barrett, Hilton; Balloun, Joseph; Weinstein, Art. (2000). Marketing Mix Factors as Moderators of the Corporate Entrepreneurship- Business Performance Relationship- A Multistage, Multivariate Analysis. *Journal of Marketing Theory and Practice.*

Bartlett, Christopher; Goshal, Sumantra. (1996). Release the Entrepreneurial Hostages from your Corporate Hierarchy. *Strategy & Leadership.* 24(4).

BBC News. (2006). Nestle Takes the World Ice Cream Lead. Retrieved: June 8, 2009. www.wikipedia.org.

BBC News. (2003). Tesco Buys Japanese Retailer. *BBC News.* Retrieved: June 8, 2009. www.wikipedia.org.

Beckett, Robert. (2003). Communication Ethics: Principle and Practice. *Journal of Communications Management.* 8(1).

Berner, Robert. (2005). Can Wal-Mart Wear a White Hat? *Business Week*. September 22, 2005. Retrieved: June 8, 2009. www.wikipedia.org.

Birkinshaw, Julian. (1997). Entrepreneurship in Multinational Corporations: The Characteristics of Subsidiary Initiatives. *Strategic Management Journal*. 18(3).

Black, Leeora; Hartel, Charmine. (2003). The Five Capabilities of Socially Responsible Companies. *Journal of Public Affairs*. 4(2).

Bloom, Matt. (2004). The Ethics of Compensation Systems. *Journal of Business Ethics*. 52(2).

Brinkmann, Johannes. (2004). Looking at Consumer Behavior in a Moral Perspective. *Journal of Business Ethics*. 51(2).

Brand Strategy. (2007). Branding in China: Building a Successful Relationship with China. *Brand Strategy*. Retrieved ProQuest: November 26, 2008. ProQuest document ID: 1286598111.

Bryant, Adam. (2009). In a Word, He Wants Simplicity. *NRF Smartbrief*. Retrieved: July 23, 2009. www.nrf.com.

Buckley, Neil. (1995). People: Leahy Rings Tesco's Tills. *Financial Times*. pg. 40. Retrieved: June 8, 2009. www.wikipedia.org.

Bulik, Beth Snyder. (2008, March). THIS BRAND MAKES YOU MORE CREATIVE. *Advertising Age*, 79(12), 4,27. Retrieved April 24, 2008, from ABI/INFORM Global database. (Document ID: 1452547301).

Bush, Michael. (2008, April 14). Coffee Klatsch 2.0. *Marketing Magazine*, pg 14.

Business Network. (2008). Retrieved: June 8, 2009. www.wikipedia.org.

Business Pundit. (2009). 10 Essential Twitter Tools for Business. *Business Pundit*. April 8, 2009. Retrieved: August 24, 2009. www.businesspundit.com.

Business Week. (2001). Viral Marketing Alert! *Business Week*. www.businessweek.com. Retrieved: June 8, 2009. www.wikipedia.org.

Business Week. (2005). Wal-Mart's British Accent Needs Polish. *Business Week*. Retrieved: November 26, 2008. http://www.businessweek.com/magazine/content/05_47/b3960070.html.

Caltrout. (2009). www.caltrout.org article. Retrieved: June 8, 2009. www.wikipedia.org.

Capio, Ralph J.; Capio, Christopher. (1998). The United States- Cuba Relationship: A Time for a Change? *Air and Space Power Journal- Chronicles Online Journal*. Retrieved: July 23, 2009. www.airpower.maxwell.af.mil.

Carrefour. (2009). Annual Results 2008. Carrefour Group. www.carrefour.com. Retrieved: June 8, 2009. www.wikipedia.org.

Cascio, Tim. (2009). Mobile Marketing: 50 Ways to Promote Your iPhone App. *Mobile Marketing, Monetization, and Methods.* June 18, 2009. Retrieved: August 24, 2009. www.timcascio.wordpress.com.

Chatterjee, Anjan; Jauchius, Matthew; Kaas, Hans-Werner; Satpathy, Aurobind. (2002). Revving up auto branding. *The McKinsey Quarterly.* 1. pp. 134-143.

Chen, Jin; Zhang, Cheng; Yuan, YuFei; Huang, Lihua. (2007). Understanding the Emerging C2C Electronic Market in China. *Electronic Markets.* 17(2). Retrieved ProQuest: November 21, 2008. ProQuest document ID: 1271721871.

Child, Peter; Heywood, Suzanne; Kliger, Michael. (2002). Do Retail Brands Travel? *The McKinsey Quarterly.* 1. pp. 11-13.

China Daily. (2004). Nestle Urged to Tell Truth About GMO's. Retrieved: June 8, 2009. www.wikipedia.org.

China Milk Scandal Claims Victim Outside Mainland. (2008). Retrieved: June 8, 2009. www.wikipedia.org.

Class PowerPoint. (2008). Dynamic Strategic Management. *Boston Consulting Growth- Share Matrix.* pg. 22.

Colchester, Max. (2007). Nescafe Brews Buzz via Blogs; Marketers are Enlisting Online Communities to Help Craft Pitches. *Wall Street Journal.* pp. 1-3. Retrieved ProQuest: May 16, 2008. ProQuest document ID: 1387169791.

Cordeiro, William. (2003). The Only Solution to the Decline in Business Ethics: Ethical Managers. *Teaching Business Ethics.* 7(3).

Corkran, Michael. (2008). Taming the Market Lion of Tomorrow. *Mergers and Acquisitions.* 43(11). Retrieved ProQuest: November 21, 2008. ProQuest document ID: 1598872141.

Corporate Watch. (2007). Unilever Environmental Pollution. *Corporate Watch.* www.corporatewatch.org.uk. Retrieved: June 8, 2009. www.wikipedia.org.

Court, David; French, Thomas; McGuire, Tim; Partington, Michael. Marketing in 3-D. *The McKinsey Quarterly.* 4. pp. 6-17.

Court, David; Leiter, Mark; Loch, Mark. (1999). Brand Leverage. *The McKinsey Quarterly* (2) 101.

Cuban Economy. (1998). Cuban Economy. *Tulane.* Retrieved: July 23, 2009. www.tulane.edu.

Cui, Geng; Choudhury, Pravat. (2003). Consumer Interests and the Ethical Implications of Marketing. *The Journal of Consumer Affairs.* 37(2).

Custom Web Express. www.customwebexpress.com. Retrieved: June 8, 2009. www.wikipedia.org.

Daboub, Anthony; Calton, Jerry. (2002). Stakeholder Learning Dialogues. *Journal of Business Ethics.* 41(1/2).

Davis, Scott; Dunn, Michael. (2002). *Building the Brand-Driven Business: Operationalize your brand to drive profitable growth.*

Destination 360. (2009). Shopping in Cuba. *Destination 360.* Retrieved: August 3, 2009. www.destination360.com.

Dickie, Mure; Nuttal, Chris. (2006). EBay Tries to Fix its Strategy in China. *Financial Times.* Retrieved ProQuest: November 21, 2008. ProQuest document ID: 1183697321.

Doebele, Justin. (2005). Standing Up to EBay. *Forbes.* Retrieved November 21, 2008. http://www.forbes.com/forbes/2005/0418/050.html.

Doing Business. (2008). Doing Business 2008. Retrieved: August 4, 2009. www.doingbusiness.com.

Duarte de Abreu Filhou, Gilberto; Calicchio, Nicola; Lunardini, Fernando (2003). Brand building in emerging markets. *The McKinsey Quarterly.* pp. 7-8.

Dumpala, Preethi. (2009). Twitter Business Tool CoTweet Raises $1.1 Million. *The Business Insider.* July 2, 2009. Retrieved: August 24, 2009. www.businessinsider.com.

Dyer, Davis; Dalzell, Frederick; Olegario, Rowena. (2004). Rising Tide: Lessons from 165 Years of Brand Building at Procter and Gamble. *Harvard Business School Press.* Retrieved: June 8, 2009. www.wikipedia.org.

Economist. (2007). Tesco Comes to America. *The Economist.* Retrieved November 27, 2008. http://www.economist.com/displaystory.cfm?story_id=9358986.

Economist. (2008). Business. *Economist.com.* Retrieved: August 3, 2009. www.economist.com.

Economy Watch. (2009). Free Market Economy. *Economy Watch.* Retrieved: July 23, 2009. www.economywatch.com.

Emery, David. (1998). Trademark of the Beast. Retrieved: June 8, 2009. www.wikipedia.org.

Emissions Study. (2008). CDP, Supply Chains, Emissions, and Climate Change. *Triple Pundit.* May 1, 2008. Retrieved: June 8, 2009. www.wikipedia.org.

Encyclopedia of Educational Technology. (2009). Behaviorism: Reinforcement and Punishment. *Encyclopedia of Educational Technology.* Retrieved: July 26, 2009. www.coe.sdsu.edu.

Encyclopedia of the Nations. (2009). Cuba- Domestic Trade. *Encyclopedia of the Nations.* Retrieved: July 23, 2009. www.nationsencyclopedia.com.

Erondu, Emmanuel; Sharland, Alex; Okpara, John. (2004). Corporate Ethics in Nigeria. *Journal of Business Ethics.* 51(4).

Eurofood. (2002). Convenience Boost for Tesco- Tesco PLC Acquires One Stop, Day and Nite Convenience Stores from T. and S. Stores PLC. *Eurofood.* Retrieved: June 8, 2009. www.wikipedia.org.

Fairclough, Gordon; Fowler, Geoffrey. (2007). Pigs Get the Ax in China. *Wall Street Journal.* pp. 1-3. Retrieved ProQuest: May 16, 2008. ProQuest document ID: 1201807851.

Ferret.com. (2008). Nestle: Global brand with Asian Signature. Retrieved: May 16, 2008. http://www.ferret.com.au.

Financial Wire Feed. (2006). EBay, TOM Online Go After Growing Chinese Market. *Financial Wire.* Retrieved ProQuest: November 21, 2008. ProQuest document ID: 1183148721.

FITA. (2009). Introduction to Cuba. *FITA.* Retrieved: July 23, 2009. www.fita.org.

Food and Drink Europe. (2005). Tesco Builds Korean Business. *Food and Drink Europe.* www.foodanddrinkeurope.com. Retrieved: June 8, 2009. www.wikipedia.org.

Food Business Review. (2008). Retrieved: June 8, 2009. www.wikipedia.org.

Foodindustry.com. (2006). Tesco Falls Foul of Slovak Government. *Foodindustry.com.* Retrieved: June 8, 2009. www.wikipedia.org.

Fortune: America's Most Admired Companies 2007. (2008). Retrieved: June 8, 2009. www.wikipedia.org.

Fox, Suzanne. (2008). China's Changing Culture and Etiquette. *The China Business Review.* 35(4). pg. 48. Retrieved ProQuest: November 26, 2008. ProQuest document ID: 1517455181.

Frank, Marc. (2009). Cuba Struggling to Pay Off Debts. *Havana Journal.* June 10, 2009. Retrieved: July 23, 2009. www.havanajournal.com.

Franks, Jeff. (2009). Castro Hints at more Belt-tightening for Cuba. *Reuters.* July 26, 2009. Retrieved: July 27, 2009. www.reuters.com.

Frey, George. (2008). The Sweet Taste of Success. *Barron's.* 88(18). pp. 18-20. Retrieved ProQuest: May 16, 2008. ProQuest document ID: 1475384951.

Frontline. (2004). The Rise of Wal-Mart. Frontline: Is Wal-Mart Good for America? www.pbs.org. Retrieved: June 8, 2009. www.wikipedia.org.

Gao, Tao. (2004). The Contingency Framework of Foreign Entry Mode Decisions. *Multinational Business Review*. 12(1).

Gaw, Bill. (2009). Customer Connectivity- The Key to Optimizing Customer Satisfaction. *Successful Office*. Retrieved: June 8, 2009. www.successfuloffice.com.

Gershon, Howard; Buerstatte. (2003). The E in Marketing: Ethics in the Age of Misbehavior. *Journal of Healthcare Management*. 48(5).

Giridharadas, A.; Rai, S. (2006). Wal-Mart to Open Hundreds of Stores in India. *The New York Times*. November 27, 2006. Retrieved: June 8, 2009. www.wikipedia.org.

Gladwell, Malcolm. (2005). *Blink. The Power of Thinking Without Thinking.* Little, Brown, and Company.

Global Powers of Retailing 2009. Deloitte and Touche. pp. 26-35.

Goett, Pamela. (1999). Michael E. Porter: A Man with a Competitive Advantage. *The Journal of Business Strategy*. pg. 2.

Goliath. (2003). Tesco to Buy Controlling Stake in Kipa. *Goliath World News*. www.goliath.ecnext.com. Retrieved: June 8, 2009. www.wikipedia.org.

Google Talking Tales. (2008). Retrieved: December 18, 2008. http://www.google.com/imgres?imgurl=http://talkingtails.files.wordpress.com/2007/07/800px-maslows_hierarchy_of_needssvg.png%3Fw%3D399%26h%3D266&imgrefurl=http://talkingtails.wordpress.com/2007/07/23/maslow-greek-philosophy-indian-mysticism/&h=524&w=800&sz=147&tbnid=ONkXJi1FwALDuM::&tbnh=94&tbnw=143&prev=/images%3Fq%3Dmaslow%2527s%2Bhierarchy%2Bof%2Bneeds%2Bpicture&hl=en&usg=__aUT71EO4f0lY_Omcy4jHnz-2R84=&sa=X&oi=image_result&resnum=1&ct=image&cd=1

Granitz, Neil. (2003). Individual, Social, and Organizational Sources of Sharing. *Journal of Business Ethics*. 42(2).

Grogg, Patricia. (2009). Economy- Cuba: Does the Ration Book Still Make Sense? *IPS News*. May 20, 2009. Retrieved: July 23, 2009. www.ipsnews.net.

Guay, Terrence; Doh, Jonathan; Sinclair, Graham. (2004). Non-Governmental Organizations, Shareholder Activism, and Socially Responsible Investments. *Journal of Business Ethics*. 52(1).

Guild, Todd. (2003). Branding's new math. *The McKinsey Quarterly 2003* (4). pg. 4.

Haar, Jerry. (2009). Cuba's Business Environment: A Risky Proposition. *Revista Inter-Forum*. Retrieved: July 23, 2009. www.revistainterforum.com.

Habiger, Sheldon. (2005). Opening the Door to China. *Functional Food & Nutraceuticals.* Retrieved ProQuest: November 26, 2008. ProQuest document ID: 940895961.

Hampton, Jack. (2009). Five Star Global Management Class PowerPoint and Discussion. July 20-22, 2009. St. John's University.

Harnick, Chris. (2009). New iPhone app launches to connect marketers. *Mobile Marketer.* August 17, 2009. Retrieved: August 24, 2009. www.mobilemarketer.com.

Helms, Marilyn. (2003. The Challenge of Entrepreneurship in a Developed Economy: The Problematic Case of Japan. *Journal of Developmental Entrepreneurship.* 8(3).

Hein, Kenneth. (2007). Teen Talk is Like, Totally Branded. *Brandweek.* 48(29). pg. 4.

Heynike, Petrae. (2008). 141st Annual general Meeting of Nestle S.A.- Speech addressed by Petrae Heynike. Retrieved: May 16, 2008. http://www.nestle.com/MediaCenter/SpeechesAndStatements.

Hirsch, Jerry. (2008). Tough Sell for Fresh & Easy. *Los Angeles Times.* Retrieved November 27, 2008. http://articles.latimes.com/2008/apr/01/business/fi-fresh1.

Hoggan, Karen. (1998). Tesco Tycoon: Interview with Tesco's Fortunes Chairman Ian MacLaurin. *Marketing.* Retrieved: June 8, 2009. www.wikipedia.org.

Hou, Jianwei. (2007). Price Determinants in Online Auctions: A Comparative Study of EBay China and US. *Journal of Electronic Commerce Research.* Retrieved ProQuest: November 21, 2008. ProQuest document ID: 1330798481.

Houston Business Journal. (2009). Report: New Twitter Tool to Monitor Business Strategy. *Houston Business Journal.* August 24, 2009. Retrieved: August 24, 2009. www.bizjournals.com.

Hughes, Jeff. (2009). App Marketing 101: Introduction to iPhone App Marketing. *148Apps.biz.* May 18, 2009. Retrieved: August 24, 2009. www.148apps.biz.

Hugues, Joublin. (2009). L'aventure du premier hyper. *L'Expansion.* Retrieved: June 8, 2009. www.wikipedia.org.

Hummels, Harry; Timmer, Diederik. (2004). Investors in Need of Social, Ethical, and Environmental Information. *Journal of Business Ethics.* 52(1).

InBev Personal Interview (2008). Doug Corbett, President InBev International. July, 2008.

Indian Coke. (2003). Indian Coke, Pepsi Laced with Pesticides, Says NGO. *Inter Press Service.* Retrieved: June 8, 2009. www.wikipedia.org.

Iyer, Gopalkrishnan. (1999). Business, Consumers and Sustainable Living in an Interconnected World. *Journal of Business Ethics.* 20(4).

Jurkiewicz, Carole; Giacalone, Robert. (2004). A Values Framework for Measuring the Impact of Workplace Spirituality on Organizational Performance. *Journal of Business Ethics.* 49(2).

Just-food. (2008). US: Wal-Mart Prepares First Marketside Openings. *Just-food.com.* Retrieved November 27, 2008. http://www.just-food.com/article.aspx?id=103867.

Karande, Kiran; Rao, CP; Singhapakdi. (2002). Moral Philosophies of Marketing Managers. *European Journal of Marketing.* 36(7/8).

Kaye, Jennifer. (2004). Coca-Cola India. *Tuck School of Business at Dartmouth.* Retrieved: June 8, 2009. www.wikipedia.org.

Kim, Chong; McInerney, Margie; Sikula, Andrew. (2004). A Model of Reasoned Responses. *Journal of Business Ethics.* 51(4).

Kimes, Mina. (2009). Fluor's Corporate Crime Fighter. *Fortune.* www.fortune.ca. Retrieved: February 9, 2009.

Knight, Gary. (2000). Entrepreneurship and Marketing Strategy: The SME Under Globalization. *Journal of International Marketing.* 8(2).

Knight, Kristina. (2009). Report: Mobile to Become Personal Advertising. *Biz Report.* August 21, 2009. Retrieved: August 24, 2009. www.bizreport.com.

Kollbrunner, Marcus. (2009). 50 Years Since the Revolution. *Socialistworld.net: website of the committee for a workers' international.* January 21, 2009. Retrieved: July 23, 2009. www.socialistworld.net.

Kraft Foods. (2002). Kraft Foods Company History. *Funding Universe.* Retrieved: June 8, 2009. www.wikipedia.org.

Kraft Personal Interview. (2008). Dino Bianco, President Kraft Canada. May, 2008.

Kraft Personal Interview. (2008). Cathy Webster. Vice President Human Resources, Kraft Canada. August 12, 2008.

Kraft Personal Interview. (2009). Dino Bianco, President Kraft Canada. August, 2009.

Kujala, Johanna. (2003). Understanding Managers' Moral Decision-Making. *International Journal of Value-Based Management.* 16(1).

Kuratko, Donald; Ireland, Duane; Hornsby, Jeffrey. (2001). Improving Firm Performance Through Entrepreneurial Actions: Acordia's Corporate Entrepreneurship Strategy. *The Academy Of Management Executive.* 15(4).

Labott, Elise. (2009). In Havana, United States turns off sign critical of Cuban government. *CNN.com.* July 27, 2009. Retrieved: July 28, 2009. www.cnn.com.

Landers, Dezmon. (2008). iPhone Apps as Marketing Tools. *StartupHustle*. July 16, 2008. Retrieved: August 24, 2009. www.startuphustle.com.

Lazar, Kay. (2004). Harvard Study Links Coca-Cola to Diabetes, Weight Gain. *Boston Herald*. www.indiaresource.org. Retrieved: January 20, 2009.

Lee, Jung-Wan; Tai, Simon. (2006). Young Consumers' Perceptions of Multinational Firms and their Acculturation Channels Towards Western Products in Transition Economies. *International Journal of Emerging Markets*. 1(3). pp. 212-220. Retrieved ProQuest: May 16, 2008. ProQuest document ID: 1139365911.

Leggatt, Helen. (2008). Twitter as a Marketing Tool? *Biz Report*. September 15, 2008. Retrieved: August, 24, 2009. www.bizreport.com.

Leggatt, Helen. (2009). E-mail Sharing via Socnets Being Overlooked by Marketers. *Biz Report*. August 20, 2009. Retrieved: August 24, 2009. www.bizreport.com.

LeVeness, Frank; Primeaux, Patrick. (2004). Vicarious Ethics: Politics, Business, and Sustainable Development. *Journal of Business Ethics*. 51(2).

Lewis, Helen. (2007). Global Market Review of New Product Development Strategies. *Just-Food*. pp. 57-81. Retrieved ProQuest: May 16, 2008. ProQuest document ID: 1400542841.

Li, Mingsheng. (2008). When in China.... *Communication World*. pg. 34. 25(6). Retrieved ProQuest: November 26, 2008. ProQuest document ID: 1595306591.

Library of Congress. (1996). Russia. *Library of Congress Country Studies*. July 31, 1996. Retrieved: August 31, 2009. www.lcweb2.loc.gov.

Liverpool Daily Post. (2006). Tesco in Poland Bid. *Liverpool Daily Post*. www.liverpooldailypost.co.uk. Retrieved: June 8, 2009. www.wikipedia.org.

Lindgreen, Adam. (2004). Corruption and Unethical Behavior. *Journal of Business Ethics*. 51(1).

Longo, Don. (2007). Gasoline a Logical Extension of Wal-Mart's Reach. *Convenience Store News*. November 1, 2007. Retrieved: June 8, 2009. www.wikipedia.org.

Lovell, Alan. (2002). Ethics as a Dependent Variable in Individual and Organizational Decision Making. *Journal of Business Ethics*. 37(2).

Lu, Jiangyong; Tao, Zhigang. (2007). EBay's Strategy in China: Alliance or Acquisition. *Asia Case Research Centre*. Class case-study.

Lumpkin, GT; Dess, Gregory. (1996). Clarifying the Entrepreneurial Orientation Construct and Linking it to Performance. *Academy of Management Review*. 21(1).

Maaruthi. (2007). The Cultural Web. *Maaruthi Wordpress.* Retrieved: July 7, 2008. www.maaruthi.wordpress.com.

Mahmud, Shahnaz. (2008, March). The Inside Job. *Adweek, 49*(11), 14-15. Retrieved April 24, 2008, from ABI/INFORM Global database. (Document ID: 1462551571).

Martin, Kirsten; Freeman, Edward. (2003). Some Problems with Employee Monitoring. *Journal of Business Ethics.* 43(4).

McAleer, Sean. (2003). Friedman's Stockholder Theory of Corporate Moral Responsibility. *Teaching Business Ethics.* 7(4).

McKinley, James. (2007). For United States Exporters in Cuba, Business Trumps Politics. *The New York Times.* November 12, 2007. Retrieved: July 23, 2009. www.nytimes.com.
McKinsey Quarterly. (2007). How half the world shops: Apparel in Brazil, China, and India. *McKinsey Quarterly.* pp. 1-13. www.mckinseyquarterly.com.
McPherson, Marianne. (2005). www.ourbodiesourselves.org. Retrieved: June 8, 2009. www.wikipedia.org.

Meacham, Jon; Thomas, Evan. (2009). Newsweek Article. *Newsweek.* February 16, 2009. Retrieved: August 3, 2009. www.newsweek.com.

Meade, Birgit; Rosen, Stacy. (1997). The Influence of Income on Global Food Spending. *Economic Research Service/ USDA.* Retrieved: May 16, 2008. http://www.ers.usda.gov.

Mendhro, Umaimah; Sinha, Abhinav. (2009). Three Keys to Staying Ethical in the Age of Madoff. *Forbes.* www.forbes.com. Retrieved: February 9, 2009.

Mittelstaedt, Fred. (2004). Research and Ethical Issues Related to Retirement Plans. *Journal of Business Ethics.* 52(2).

Montgomery, Alan. (2001). Applying Quantitative Marketing Techniques to the Internet. *Interfaces.* 31(2). Retrieved: June 8, 2009. www.wikipedia.org.

Morningnewsbeat.com. (2009. Retrieved: June 9, 2009. www.morningnewsbeat.com.

Morrow, JL. (2002). Someone Old or Someone New?: The Effects of CEO Change on Corporate Entrepreneurship. *New England Journal of Entrepreneurship.* 5(2).

MSNBC. (2005). Is Wal-Mart Going Green? MSNBC. October 25, 2005. www.msnbc.com. Retrieved: June 8, 2009. www.wikipedia.org.

MSNBC. (2006). Wal-Mart Turns Attention to Upscale Shoppers. *MSNBC.* March 23, 2006. Retrieved: June 8, 2009. www.wikipedia.org.

Mullen, Megan Gwynne. (2003). A Scheduling and Programming Innovator. *The Rise of Cable Programming in the United States: Revolution or Evolution?* www.books.google.com. Retrieved: June 8, 2009. www.wikipedia.org.

Murphy, James. (2007). Struggling EBay Inks TOM Deal. *Media.* Retrieved ProQuest: November 21, 2008. ProQuest document ID: 1212323951.

Nadu, Tamil. (2004). Incidence of Diabetes in India Underestimated. *The Hindu.* www.hindu.com. Retrieved: January 20, 2009.

Nestle SA website. (2008). Retrieved: December 22, 2008. http://www.nestle.com/Brands/Brands.html

Nestle SA website. (2008). Financial Statements 2008. www.nestle.com. Retrieved: June 8, 2009. www.wikipedia.com.

Nestle Investor Relations. (2008). Nestle Management Report 2007.

Nestle Personal Interview. (2008). Bob Leonidas, President Nestle Canada. May 12, 2008.

Nestle Personal Interview. (2008). Bob Leonidas, President Nestle Canada. August 5, 2008.

Nestle Personal Interview. (2009). Bob Leonidas, President Nestle Canada. August 2, 2009.

Nestle Press Release. (2002). Nestle and Ethiopia: A Statement by Nestle CEO Peter Brabeck. Retrieved: June 8, 2009. www.wikipedia.org.

Nestle Public Affairs. (2008). The Nestle Creating Shared Value Report.

Nestle UK Partners Blend. (2007). About Our Brands. Nestle.co.uk. Retrieved: June 8, 2009. www.wikipedia.org.

New York Times. (1996). Unilever Agrees to Buy Helene Curtis. New York Times. Retrieved: June 8, 2009. www.wikipedia.org.

Nielsen. (2009). Walmart Mid-Year Review. *Nielsen.* Special Report July, 2009.

NIVEA: Widespread allure. (2007, September). *Marketing Week,26.* Retrieved May 16, 2008, from ABI/INFORM Global database. (Document ID: 1335546331).

NPR Article. (2008). In Cairo Slum, the Poor Spark Environmental Change. *NPR.* April 27, 2008. Retrieved: June 8, 2009. www.wikipedia.org.

Oates, John. (2007). Amazon Ups Spending In China. *Financial News.* Retrieved November 21, 2008. http://www.theregister.co.uk/2007/06/05/amazon_china/print.html.

On Facebook, Ad Sales and the Games People Play. (2008, March). *MIN's B 2 B, 11*(8), pg 1. Retrieved April 24, 2008, from ABI/INFORM Trade & Industry database. (Document ID: 1438450941).

Ong, Rebecca. (2008). Doing Business 2008: Making a Difference. *International Finance Corporation: Creating Opportunity*. Retrieved: August 3, 2009. www.ifc.org.

Orr, Deborah. (2006). Slave Chocolate? Retrieved: June 8, 2009. www.wikipedia.org.

Oxford English Dictionary. (2008). http://www.en.wikipedia.org/wiki/Brand. Retrieved April 26, 2008.

Peng, Yusheng. (2004). Kinship networks and Entrepreneurs in China's Transitional Economy. *The American Journal of Sociology.* 109(5).

Pepsico Article. Retrieved: June 8, 2009. www.wikipedia.org.

PepsiCo Personal Interview. (2008). Interview with Marc Guay, President of Pepsico Canada. August 11, 2008.

Pepsico Personal Interview. (2009). Interview with Donna Hrinak, Senior Director, Latin America Government Affairs, Pepsico. September 3, 2009.

Pepsico Press Release. (2009). Pepsico Agrees to Acquire Amacoco, Brazil's Largest Water Company. Retrieved: August 12, 2009. www.finance.yahoo.com.

PepsiCo Program Sessions. (2005). Pepsico International Program Sessions. October 12-13, 2005.

Pepsico Values Guide. (2008).
Pet Food and Pet Care Products in Venezuela. (2008). Retrieved: June 8, 2009. www.wikipedia.org.
Planet Retail. (2009). Daily News by Planet Retail. Retrieved: June 23, 2009. www.planetretail.net.

Planet Retail. (2009). Daily News by Planet Retail. Retrieved: July 1, 2009. www.planetretail.net.

Planet Retail. (2009). Daily News by Planet Retail. Retrieved: August 19, 2009. www.planetretail.net.

Planet Retail. (2009). Daily News by Planet Retail. Retrieved: August 24, 2009. www.planetretail.net.

Planet Retail. (2009). Global Channel Strategies. *Planet Retail Global Trends Report.* Planet Retail Limited. London, UK.

Premeaux, Shane. (2004). The Current Link Between Management Behavior and Ethical Philosophy. *Journal of Business Ethics.* 51(3).

Price Chopper Branding PowerPoint. (2009).

Procter and Gamble Annual Report. (2008). Letter from A.G. Lafley. Retrieved: June 8, 2009. www.wikipedia.org.

Procter and Gamble Document. (2005). Finding Alternatives for Product Safety Testing. *Procter and Gamble Publication.* www.wikipedia.org.

Procter and Gamble Personal Interview. (2008). Tim Penner, President Procter and Gamble Canada.

Procter and Gamble's Purpose, Values, and Principles. (2008).

Qin, Juying. (2007). TOM Online to Shop for Success in China. *Wall Street Journal.* Retrieved ProQuest: November 21, 2008. ProQuest document ID: 1204445671.

Quenqua, Douglas. (2008). Study: Majority Use Social Media to "Vent" About Customer Care. *The ClickZ Network.* pg. 1.

Radwan, Sam. (2008). Exporting Growth Strategies. *Best's Review.* 108(9). Retrieved ProQuest: November 26, 2008. ProQuest document ID: 1412236901.

Renton, Jennifer; Binedell, Nick. (2002). World Marketing Guru Kevin Lane Keller Presents Lessons on Strategic Brand Management. *Gale Group PR Newswire.* pp. 1-2.

Reuters. (2008). Tesco to Buy Thirty-Six South Korean Stores. *Reuters.* www.uk.reuters.com. Retrieved: June 8, 2009. www.wikipedia.org.

Roberts, Dexter; Rocks, David. (2005). Let a Thousand Brands Bloom. *Business Week.* Issue 3955. pp. 58-62. Retrieved ProQuest: May 16, 2008. ProQuest document ID: 910537261.

Romar, Edward. (2004). Managerial Harmony: The Confucian Ethics of Peter F. Drucker. *Journal of Business Ethics.* 51(2).

Rowley, Jennifer. (2004). Online Branding. *Online Information Review.* 28(2). pg. 131.

Ruettgers, Mike. (2003). Responsibility Lies in Leadership. *Vital Speeches of the Day.* 70(5).

Sacramento Business Journal. (2008). Analyst: Tesco's Fresh & Easy Stores in Trouble. *Sacramento Business Journal.* Retrieved November 27, 2008. http://www.bizjournals.com/sacramento/stories/2008/03/10/daily57.html?ana=from_rss.

Sama, Linda; Shoaf, Victoria. (2002). Ethics on the Web. *Journal of Business Ethics.* 36(1/2).

Schindehutte, Minet; Morris, Michael; Kuratko, Donald. (2000). Triggering Events, Corporate Entrepreneurship and the Marketing Function. *Journal of Marketing Theory and Practice.* 8(2).

Schultz, Don. (2002, Sept/ Oct). Who Owns the Brand? *Marketing Management, (11)*5, pg 9.

Schwepker, Charles. (2003). An Exploratory Investigation of the Relationship Between Ethical Conflict and Salesperson Performance. *The Journal of Business and Industrial Marketing.* 18(4/5).

Sell, Hannah. (2009). Socialism in the Twenty-First Century. *Socialist Party- World Analysis.* Retrieved: August 2, 2009. www.socialistparty.com.

Shackelford, David. (2009). Facebook Groups: E-Mail Marketing, Evolved. *Shack Attack: Social Media.* April 24, 2009. Retrieved: August 21, 2009. www.dshack.net.

Shaw, Deirdre; Shiu, Edward. (2003). Ethics in Consumer Choice. *European Journal of Marketing.* 37(10).

ShopSavvy. (2009). The final frontier: Groceries! *ShopSavvy.* April 8, 2009. Retrieved: August 21, 2009. www.biggu.com.

Simms, Jane. (2007, December). Brands we love... ...and brands we hate. *Marketing,* 51-52. Retrieved April 24, 2008, from ABI/INFORM Global database. (Document ID: 1415779871).

Simons, Ross. (2008). The Four Levers of Control. Retrieved July 5, 2008. http://maaruthi.wordpress.com/2007/06/10/the-cultural-web/.

Singh, Navjit. (2008). Corporate Strategy: Best Practice- Perfect Landing. *Foreign Direct Investment.* Retrieved ProQuest: November 21, 2008. ProQuest document ID: 1574165971.

SinoCast China (2007). EBay CEO Has Something to Say About Free Policy. *SinoCast China Business Daily News.* Retrieved ProQuest: November 21, 2008. ProQuest document ID: 1301704891.

SinoCast China (2007). EBay Confident in JV with TOM Online. *SinoCast China Business Daily News.* Retrieved ProQuest: November 21, 2008. ProQuest document ID: 1232016671.

SinoCast China. (2007). Former eBay China President Joins Matrix Partners. *SinoCast China Business Daily News.* Retrieved ProQuest: November 21, 2008. ProQuest document ID: 1292628341.
SinoCast China (2007). Google China to Have 500-Plus Employees at Year-End. *SinoCast China Business Daily News.* Retrieved ProQuest: November 21, 2008. ProQuest document ID: 1290392381.

Snell, Robin; Herndon, Neil. (2004). Hong Kong's Code of Ethics Initiative. *Journal of Business Ethics.* 51(1).

Snopes. (2007). Coca-Cola and Israel. www.snopes.com. Retrieved: June 8, 2009. www.wikipedia.org.

Sparkes, Russell; Cowton, Christopher. (2004). The Maturing of Socially Responsible Investment. *Journal of Business Ethics.* 52(1).

Spickett-Jones, Graham; Kitchen, Philip; Reast, Jon. (2003). Social Facts and Ethical Hardware. *Journal of Communication Management.* 8(1).

Sporting Clube de Portugal. (2009). Retrieved: June 8, 2009. www.wikipedia.org.

Srnka, Katharina. (2004). Culture's Role in Marketers' Ethical Decision Making. *Academy of Marketing Science Review.*

Stovall, Scott; Neill, John; Perkins, David. (2004). Corporate Governance, Internal Decision Making, and the Invisible Hand. *Journal of Business Ethics.* 51(2).

Supermarket News. (2009). Wal-Mart Debuts Club Store for Hispanics. *Supermarket News.* Retrieved: August 10, 2009. www.supermarketnews.com.

Tamayo, Juan. (2009). Less Phones Per Capita in Cuba Now Than in 1958. *Havana Journal.* July 23, 2009. Retrieved: July 23, 2009. www.havanajournal.com.

Taylor, Charles. (2008). Lifestyle Matters Everywhere- Marketers Need to Stop Targeting Consumers by Country and Instead Target Based on Habits, Likes, Dislikes. *AdAge.com.* pp. 1-5. Retrieved: May 20, 2008. http://adage.com/cmostrategy.

Tesco (2006). Tesco Announces Non-Food Store Trials. Tesco. www.tescocorporate.com. Retrieved: June 8, 2009. www.wikipedia.org.

Tesco. (2008). Tesco Careers- Human Resources. Tesco. www.tesco-graduates.com. Retrieved: June 8, 2009. www.wikipedia.org.

Tesco. (2006). Tesco DVD Rental. Tesco. www.tescodvdrental.com. Retrieved: June 8, 2009. www.wikipedia.org.

Tesco. (2006). Tesco Our History. Tesco PLC. www.tescocorporate.com. Retrieved: June 8, 2009. www.wikipedia.org.

Tesco Hungary. (2008). Tesco Services. Tesco Hungary. www.tesco.hu. Retrieved: June 8, 2009. www.wikipedia.org.

Tesco Lotus. (2008). Key Facts About Tesco Lotus. Tesco Lotus. www.tescolotus.net. Retrieved: June 8, 2009. www.wikipedia.org.

Tesco Personal Interview. August 3, 2009. Daniel Gilsenan, Director of Business Development, Tesco.

Tesco Poland. (2008). About Tesco Poland. Tesco Poland. www.tesco.pl. Retrieved; June 8, 2009. www.wikipedia.org.

That Which People Eat. (2009).

The Economist. (2007). No Ketchup, Please. *The Economist.* www.economist.com. Retrieved: June 8, 2009. www.wikipedia.org.

The Guardian. (2007). PDF of The 2006 Giving List. *The Guardian.* www.image.guardian.co.uk. Retrieved: June 6, 2009. www.wikipedia.org.

The Guardian. (2009). Tesco Unveils Record Profits of 3 Billion Pounds. *The Guardian.* April, 2009. Retrieved: June 8, 2009. www.wikipedia.org.

The Times. (2008). Monday Manifesto: Unilever Chairman Michael Treschow. *The Times.* May 26, 2008.

The Times. (2008). Tesco Express Rolls Into China. *The Times.* www.business.timesonline.co.uk. Retrieved: June 8, 2009. www.wikipedia.org.

Third World Traveler. (1997). A Historical Look at the Pepsico/ Burma Boycott. *Third World Traveler.* www.thirdworldtraveler.com. Retrieved: June 8, 2009. www.wikipedia.org.

Thomasson, Emma. (2009). Nestlé's Nespresso Sees Double Digit Sales Growth. *Reuters.com.* Retrieved: June 10, 2009.

Thornberry, Neal. (2003). Corporate Entrepreneurship: Teaching Managers to be Entrepreneurs. *The Journal of Management Development.* 22(4).

Thuermer, Karen E. (2007, August). Cover Story: Cobra Beer - From small beer. *Foreign Direct Investment,*1. Retrieved May 16, 2008, from ABI/INFORM Global database. (Document ID: 1320281921).

Tong, Tony; Reuer, Jeffrey; Peng, Mike. (2008). International Joint Ventures and the Value of Growth Options. *Academy of Management Journal.* 51(5). Retrieved ProQuest: November 21, 2008. ProQuest document ID: 1594616781.

Travel Document Systems. (2009). Cuba North America. *Travel Document Systems.* Retrieved: July 23, 2009. www.traveldocs.com.

Trunick, Perry. (2006). Wal-Mart Reinvents Itself in China. *Newsweek.* October 30, 2006. Retrieved: June 8, 2009. www.wikipedia.org.

Tucker, Robert. (2002). Adding Value Profitability. *The American Salesman.*

TweetPR. (2009). Debunking the Social Media Barriers. *TweetPR.* Retrieved: August 21, 2009. www.tweetpr.com.

Unilever. (2008). Unilever has announced its intention to have all of its palm oil certified sustainable by 2015. www.unilever.com. Retrieved: June 8, 2009. www.wikipedia.org.

Unilever Annual Report. (2008). Annual Report. Retrieved: June 8, 2009. www.wikipedia.org.

Unilever Disrobed. (2008). Unilever Disrobed: Interview with Dove/ Axe Mashup Artist. Retrieved: June 8, 2009. www.wikipedia.org.

Unilever Heartbrand. (2006). Unilever Heartbrand. Retrieved: June 8, 2009. www.wikipedia.org.

Unilever Personal Interview. (2008). Jeffrey Allgrove, Senior Vice President Unilever Brand Integration. July 29, 2008.

Unilever Personal Interview. (2009). David Blanchard, President Unilever Canada. August 10, 2009.

Unilever Powerpoint. (2009). Document presented to Price Chopper May, 2009.

United States Bureau of Western Hemisphere Affairs. (2008). Background Note: Cuba. *Bureau of Western Hemisphere Affairs: United States Department of State.* Retrieved: July 23, 2009. www.state.gov.

University of Massachusetts Amherst study. (2006). Political Economy Research Institute Toxic 100. Retrieved: June 8, 2009. www.wikipedia.org.

USA Today. (2005). Viral Advertising Spreads Through Marketing Plans. *USA Today.* www.usatoday.com. Retrieved: June 8, 2009. www.wikipedia.org.

USDA. (2008). http://www.ers.usda.gov/publications/agoutlook/jul1997/ao242e.pdf. pg. 14. Retrieved May 16, 2008.

Valentine, Sean; Godkin, Lynn; Lucero, Margaret. (2002). Ethical Context, Organizational Commitment, and Person-Organization Fit. *Journal of Business Ethics.* 41(4).

Velasquez, Manuel. (2001). *Business Ethics: Concepts and Cases (5th Edition).* Prentice Hall.

Walden, Jamie. (2008). Confucius Institute Helps Arkansas Companies Go Global. *Arkansas Business.* 25(41). pg. 16. Retrieved ProQuest: November 26, 2008. ProQuest document ID: 1590508371.

Wallis, William; Mahtani, Dino. (2007). Ivory Coast: Cocoa Exports Fund Ivory Coast Conflict. Retrieved: June 8, 2009. www.wikipedia.org.

Wal-Mart Annual Report. (2006). Wal-Mart 2006 Annual Report. *Wal-Mart.* Retrieved: June 8, 2009. www.wikipedia.org.

Wal-Mart Facts. (2006). The Wal-Mart Timeline. www.walmartfacts.com. Retrieved: June 8, 2009. www.wikipedia.org.

Wal-Mart SEC. (2006). Wal-Mart SEC Form 10-K. *United States Securities and Exchange Commission.* January 31, 2006. Retrieved: June 8, 2009. www.wikipedia.org.

Wal-Mart Watch. (2008). Shareholder Information. www.walmartwatch.com. Retrieved: February 11, 2009.

Waring, Peter; Lewer, John. (2004). The Impact of Socially Responsible Investment on Human Resource Management. *Journal of Business Ethics.* 52(1).

Watson, Tony. (2003). Ethical Choice in Managerial Work. *Human Relations.* 56(2).

Weiss, Gregory. (1999). An Investment in Coca-Cola will be the Real Thing. *Investment Quality Trends.* www.thebullandbear.com. Retrieved: January 20, 2009.

Wherrity, Constance. (2006). Dial Agrees to Buy Procter and Gamble Deodorant Brands. *Pierce Mattie Public Relations New York blog.* www.piercemattie.com. Retrieved: June 8, 2009. www.wikipedia.org.

Wikipedia. (2009). Carrefour. Retrieved: June 8, 2009. www.wikipedia.org.

Wikipedia. (2009). Kraft. Retrieved: June 8, 2009. www.wikipedia.org.

Wikipedia. (2009). Nestle. Retrieved: June 8, 2009. www.wikipedia.org.
Wikipedia. (2009). Social Media. Retrieved: June 8, 2009. www.wikipedia.org.

Wikipedia. (2009). Tesco. Retrieved: June 8, 2009. www.wikipedia.org.

Wikipedia. (2009). Wal-Mart. Retrieved: June 8, 2009. www.wikipedia.org.

Wired. (2005). Marketers Feverish Over Viral Ads. www.wired.com. Retrieved: June 8, 2009. www.wikipedia.org.

Wood, Stuart. (2006). Brand Continuity: It's the same, but different. *Brand Strategy.* pp. 1-3. Retrieved ProQuest: May 16, 2008. ProQuest document ID: 1060502761.

Woodall, Katherine. (2002). Survival- Can Branding Save Your Organization? *Communication World.* pp. 11-12.

Wordnet.princeton.edu/perl/webwn. Retrieved April 26, 2008.

World Health Organization Fact Sheet. (2008). What is Diabetes? www.who.int. Retrieved: January 20, 2009.

World Socialist Movement. (2009). How the WSM is Different from Other Groups. *The World Socialist Movement.* Retrieved: August 3, 2009. www.worldsocialism.org.

www.answers.com. Retrieved: January 31, 2009.

www.wordnet.princeton.edu. Retrieved: January 31, 2009.

Yahoo Finance. (2009). Breyers Premieres Latest Webisode Parody Starring Jane Krakowski. *Yahoo Finance*. Retrieved: June 10, 2009. www.finance.yahoo.com.

Yahoo Finance. (2009). Doritos Breaks New Ground in Fusing Music and Technology by putting Blink-182, big Boi Concerts in the Palms of Fans' Hands. *Yahoo Finance*. Retrieved: July 6, 2009. www.finance.yahoo.com.

Yahoo Finance. (2009). Key Facts About Russia's Retail Sector. *Yahoo Finance- Reuters*. September 3, 2009. Retrieved: September 3, 2009. www.reuters.com.

Yahoo Finance. (2009). Russian Equities Could Soar Amid Government Support, Steady Oil. *Yahoo Finance*. September 3, 2009. Retrieved: September 3, 2009. www.finance.yahoo.com.

Yahoo Finance. (2009). Starbucks Ice Cream Invites Facebook to Treat Friends and Family. *Yahoo Finance*. Retrieved: July 6, 2009. www.finance.yahoo.com.

Yahoo Finance. (2009). Wal-Mart Stores, Inc. *Yahoo Finance*. www.finance.yahoo.com. Retrieved: June 8, 2009. www.wikipedia.org.

Yeung, Matthew; Ramasamy, Bala. (2008). Brand value and firm performance nexus: Further empirical evidence. *Journal of Brand Management, 15(5)*, 322-335. Retrieved April 24, 2008, from ABI/INFORM Global database. (Document ID: 1459651371).

Yuthas, Kristi; Dillard, Jesse; Rogers, Rodney. (2004). Beyond Agency and Structure. *Journal of Business Ethics*. 51(2).

Zook, Matthew; Graham, Mark. (2006). Wal-Mart Nation: Mapping the Reach of a Retail Colossus. *Wal-Mart World: The World's Biggest Corporation in the Global Economy*. pp. 15-25. Retrieved: June 8, 2009. www.wikipedia.org.

Zyglidopolous, Stelios. (2002). The Social and Environmental Responsibilities of Multinationals. *Journal of Business Ethics*. 36(1/2).

24/7 Wall Street. (2009). The Future of Twitter- 10 Ways Twitter Will Change American Business. 24/7 Wall St. August 24, 2009. Retrieved: August 24, 2009. www.time.com

Endnotes

1 Renton, Binedell, 2002
2 Lewis, 2007
3 Lee and Tai, 2006
4 Aisner, 2000
5 Court, French, McGuire, and Partington, 1999
6 Davis and Dunn, 2002
7 Ibid.
8 Ibid.
9 Chatterjee, Jauchius, Kaas, and Satpathy, 2002
10 Rowley, 2004
11 Ibid.
12 Oxford English Dictionary, 2008
13 Wordnet, 2006
14 Quenqua, 2008
15 Simms, 2007
16 Ibid.
17 Wood, 2006
18 Ibid.
19 Ibid.
20 Child, Heywood, and Kliger, 2002
21 McKinsey Quarterly, 2007
22 Ibid.
23 Ibid.
24 Ibid.
25 Ibid.
26 Global Powers of Retailing, 2009
27 Ibid.
28 Ibid.
29 Ibid.
30 That Which People Eat, 2009
31 Planet Retail, 2009
32 Ibid.
33 Ibid.
34 Ibid.
35 Ibid.
36 Ibid.
37 Ibid.
38 Ibid.
39 Ibid.
40 Ibid.
41 Nielsen, 2009
42 Nestle SA website, 2008
43 Wikipedia, 2008
44 BBC News, 2006
45 Food Business Review, 2009
46 Lewis, 2007
47 Auto News, 2007
48 Nestle Public Affairs, 2008
49 Nestle website, 2008
50 Frey, 2008
51 Anonymous, 2008
52 Nestle website, 2008

[53] Heynike, 2008
[54] Ball, 2007
[55] Ferret.com, 2008
[56] Nestle Management Report, 2007
[57] Nestle UK- Partners Blend, 2007
[58] Nestle Press Release, 2002
[59] Pet Food and Pet Care Products in Venezuela, 2008
[60] Wikipedia, 2009
[61] Caltrout, 2009
[62] China Daily, 2004
[63] Orr, 2006
[64] Wallis and Mahtani, 2007
[65] China Milk, 2008
[66] Nestle Personal Interview, 2008
[67] Thomasson, 2009
[68] Fortune, 2007
[69] Dyer, Dalzell, Olegario, 2004
[70] Wherrity, 2006
[71] Procter and Gamble Annual Report, 2008
[72] Emery, 1998
[73] McPherson, 2005
[74] Custom Web Express
[75] UMass Study, 2006
[76] Business Network, 2008
[77] Emissions Study, 2008
[78] NPR Article, 2008
[79] P&G Document, 2005
[80] Roberts and Rocks, 2005
[81] P&G Personal Interview, 2008
[82] P&G Purpose, Values, and Principles, 2008
[83] Davis and Dunn, 2002
[84] AB InBev Personal Interview with Doug Corbett, 2008
[85] AB InBev Personal Interview with Steve Burrows, 2008
[86] Unilever Annual Report, 2008
[87] Unilever Power Point, 2009
[88] New York Times, 1996
[89] Unilever Heartbrand, 2006
[90] Unilever, 2008
[91] Unilever Power Point, 2009
[92] Corporate Watch, 2007
[93] Unilever Disrobed, 2008
[94] Unilever PowerPoint, 2009
[95] The Times, 2008
[96] Unilever PowerPoint, 2009
[97] Woodall, 2002
[98] Abreu Filho, Calicchio, and Lunardini, 2003
[99] Unilever Personal Interview Jeffrey Allgrove, 2008
[100] Wikipedia, 2009
[101] Kraft Foods, 2002
[102] The Economist, 2009
[103] Wikipedia, 2009
[104] Kraft Personal Interview, Dino Bianco, 2009
[105] Kraft Personal Interview, Cathy Webster, 2009
[106] PepsiCo Article, 2009

[107] PepsiCo Personal Interview, Marc Guay, 2009
[108] PepsiCo Values, 2005
[109] Kaye, 2004
[110] India Coke, 2003
[111] Third World Traveler, 1997
[112] Snopes, 2007
[113] PepsiCo, 2009
[114] Price Chopper Branding PowerPoint, 2009
[115] Ibid.
[116] Tesco, 2006.
[117] The Guardian, 2009
[118] Tesco, 2006
[119] Hoggan, 1998
[120] Buckley, 1995
[121] Eurofood, 2002
[122] BBC News, 2003
[123] Goliath, 2003
[124] Liverpool Daily Post, 2006
[125] Tesco, 2006
[126] The Times, 2008
[127] Tesco, 2008
[128] Tesco Hungary, 2008
[129] Tesco, 2008
[130] Foodindustry.com, 2006
[131] Food and Drink, 2005
[132] Reuters, 2008
[133] Tesco, 2008
[134] Planet Retail, 2009
[135] Tesco, 2008
[136] The Guardian, 2006
[137] Wikipedia, 2009
[138] Tesco, 2009
[139] Wikipedia, 2009
[140] Carrefour, 2009
[141] Wikipedia, 2009
[142] Hugues, 2009
[143] Wikipedia, 2009
[144] Planet Retail, 2009
[145] Ibid.
[146] Yahoo Finance, 2009
[147] Frontline, 2004
[148] Walmart Facts, 2006
[149] Zook, Graham, 2006
[150] Nielsen, 2009
[151] Ibid.
[152] MSNBC, 2005
[153] Berner, 2005
[154] MSNBC, 2006
[155] Walmart, 2008
[156] Longo, 2007
[157] Planet Retail, 2009
[158] Walmart, 2008
[159] Asda, 2007
[160] Walmart, 2006

[161] Walmart, 2007
[162] Giridharadas, Rai, 2006
[163] Attwood, 2009
[164] Planet Retail, 2009
[165] Nielsen, 2009
[166] Trunick, 2006
[167] Barbaro, 2007
[168] Planet Retail, 2009
[169] Bryant, 2009
[170] Gaw, 2009
[171] Anonymous, 2005
[172] Davis and Dunn, 2002
[173] United States Department of Agriculture, 2008
[174] Premeux, 2004
[175] Weiss, 1999
[176] World Health Organization Fact Sheet, 2008
[177] Lazar, 2004
[178] Nadu, 2004
[179] Anonymous, 2009
[180] Business Week, 2005
[181] Economist, 2007
[182] Sacramento Business Journal, 2008
[183] Hirsch, 2008
[184] Just-Food, 2008
[185] Anonymous, 2008
[186] Li, 2008
[187] Walden, 2008
[188] Fox, 2008
[189] SupermarketNews, 2009
[190] Nielsen, 2009
[191] Woodall, 2002
[192] Personal Interview AB InBev Steve Burrows, 2009
[193] Woodall, 2002
[194] Guild, 2003
[195] Ibid.
[196] Chatterjee, Jauchius, Kaas, and Satpathy, 2002
[197] Court, French, McGuire, and Partington, 1999
[198] Chatterjee, Jauchius, Kaas, and Satpathy, 2002
[199] Woodall, 2002
[200] Davis, Dunn, 2002
[201] Taylor, 2008
[202] Court, French, McGuire, and Partington, 1999
[203] Wood, 2006
[204] Davis and Dunn, 2002
[205] Ibid.
[206] Abreu Filho, Calicchio, and Lunardini, 2003
[207] Tucker, 2002
[208] Goett, 1999
[209] Boston Consulting Matrix
[210] Simons, 2008
[211] Bulik, 2008
[212] Rowley, 2004
[213] Davis and Dunn, 2002
[214] Court, Leiter, and Loch, 1999

[215] Schultz, 2002
[216] Davis and Dunn, 2002
[217] Abreu Filho, Calicchio, and Lunardini, 2003
[218] Yeung, Ramasamay, 2008
[219] Davis and Dunn, 2008
[220] Court, Leiter, Loch, 1999
[221] Schultz, 2002

Made in the USA
San Bernardino, CA
22 April 2016